# Todmorden Album 4

Roger Birch

# Todmorden Album 4

*People Places and Events*

## Roger Birch

*Foreword by* Glyn Hughes

The Woodlands Press

First published in 2006 by
The Woodlands Press
General Wood
Todmorden
West Yorkshire OL14 6QE

Copyright © Roger Birch 2006
Introduction © Glyn Hughes 2006

All rights reserved

ISBN 0-9509100-3-1

British Library Cataloguing-in-Publication Data
A catalogue record for this book is available from the British Library

Printed and bound in Verona, Italy

*Frontispiece:* Temperance Street, 1973

# Foreword

I was in one town in Calderdale a year ago when an old Landrover pulled up. If it had been well kept it might have been called "classic", but this was an old and mistreated workhorse, its canvas top torn, it's sides battered. At five miles per hour, the poor thing screeched to a halt on what was left of the metal studs of its brakes. Out tumbles an old farmer of the hills. How did I know that? It was unmistakable – the old, brown slop-coat, the mired wellingtons, the dreadful dentistry – except that, untypically, he was laughing his head off, and all but rolling on the pavement. Some kind of especial jubilance caused him to spill over into a most curious sense of camaraderie. He caught my eye and shouted, "Tha should be cheerful! Tha should be allus laughing, like me!" "I'm a poet," I replied. "I'm supposed to be miserable." It turned out that he had sold his collapsing barn and cowshed, just in time before it fell down. (But would that have made any difference to the price?) He could not contain his amazement and delight. I'm not surprised. Think of his and his ancestors' years of milking cows on dark, freezing mornings, of making hay between the bleak rains, and staring without profit or help into the dreary mists … no wonder he was consumed with mirth.

Doubtless he would never understand the why or wherefore of it, but should he look a gift horse in the mouth? I wonder, though, if he was one of the many who, when up to the neck in depression and poverty, lamented that "the hippies" (or, even worse, lesbians and gays) "are taking over"? Ironically, it was these at-the-time equally penurious newcomers, combined with general social factors such as motorways and the perceived-fearfulness of living in cities, that brought about the change, one so financially beneficial to any who held on to property and assets. Environmentally beneficial too. Ironically, it was these apparent drifters who largely inspired and led the preservation of what still survived from the past.

You might think there had never been a revolution before, with its pathos and its laments. In fact, fifty or one hundred years before photography and before the earliest images in this book, there came what seemed at the time as big a catastrophe (or "improvement", depending on how you look at it) as anything appearing to our apocalyptic eyes in the late twentieth early twenty first centuries. When studying the productive twinning of industrial development and nonconformity of that period, what struck me was that it was largely powered by erstwhile itinerant wanderers similar in attitude to those who recently have been despised as "hippies".

I offer this summary because the most striking aspect of the photographs in this book, portraying a period from the first general use of photography to the point of change in the nineteen seventies, is how clearly that one hundred years was a single, consistent age. The earliest pictures belong recognisably to the same world as the most recent. It was an age that ended as suddenly and brutally as a train hitting the bumpers; and since 1970, it has seemed as distant as if it existed one thousand years ago. It isn't that surviving buildings and streets have altered so radically, nor the fields and hills. It is the life that is lived in them or on them that has changed – the outlook, the philosophy. Above all, the relationships between people. That different outlook, which for better or for worse we have lost, is common to every face, on every street-corner and hayfield, in these photographs. It is an attitude as strange to us, infested as we are with globalised journalism, as if it all took place on the moon. They all announce by their expressions that they *belong* to this place, its weather, its history, its geography, and its hills … and to each other. The Brontës would not have found it over-strange.

By contrast, a harsh view of my contemporaries here might claim that many care for little more than the possession of a safe condominium, somewhere to graze ponies for the kids, and for good transport out of the place.

(And also, I suspect, the Brontës would have found this modern world more congenial. I can see the snobbish Charlotte enjoying her off-roader, as she enjoyed travelling first-class to London and her expensive teas. I can imagine Emily enjoying the wilder reaches of the Internet. Branwell would have been totally at home with "hippies".)

Todmorden (unalterably, I hope) is like few other places. Some Welsh mining and slate-quarrying towns are similar, but nowhere else is in the Calder Valley, quite. The shut-in bleakness especially where the valleys struggle towards Bacup and Burnley. The industrial scarring of the hills. Its character is powerfully expressed in the dark tones of these photographs. Its dark nature … the "genius" of the place … is I suggest older than industry, and ancient. I have speculated, maybe fancifully, that the very name, Todmorden, derives from two words for "death". "Tod" and "mor" (as in "mort"): "Death-death-wood." John Billingsley, our local mythologist and pre-historian, claims that the place names in the three valleys converging in Todmorden show that they were occupied by different tribes.

But isn't part of its charm this "character" that can never quite be eradicated? I have a friend who moved recently from Hebden Bridge to Todmorden because, he felt, Todmorden still held the quality that Hebden Bridge has managed to erase, now becoming bland. Todmorden is at present surging with the energies of mixed people, those who have been here for generations, and incomers. This makes its market and its shops a delight. I hope Todmorden continues, both to preserve its historical self, but also to continue being vital.

There are many streets and buildings shown here, and it is remarkable (considering what has happened to most places) how little of this splendour, or at any rate its local aptness, has been lost. The now architecturally abhorred period of the fifties to the nineties did not *quite* pass Todmorden by, but it did have relatively little impact. It has been remarked that the Calder Valley is too geographically stubborn to be drastically altered. I'm not sure how true this is – though certainly it is difficult to sprawl very far. Perhaps it is truer that the rock-like endurance has entered into the spirit of people?

I find in these photographs yet another extraordinary lack of change. What one normally observes is that, circa nineteen twenty, people learned that it is permissible to smile on camera. It came as a consequence of faster exposure times, and the invention of the handy, Kodak Box-Brownie camera. This was quite a social revolution. (The digital camera will be bringing about a further revolution in casualness today. I wonder what miracles for future archivists are even now being stored on home computers?) Gone, the frozen stage-sets of the Victorians and

Edwardians. In fact it became *mandatory* to smile for the camera. That change also seems, judging by these pictures, to have passed Todmorden by. They pose outside their premises expressing the fact that they have serious business on hand, whether they are the tenants of The Shepherds Rest pub, or proprietors of Gatley's electrical engineering business, "the first of its kind in Todmorden", a butcher's or a draper's. Instead of spontaneous cheerfulness, they are often composed in groups with a stateliness very fitting for their grand, Victorian, and rocky backgrounds. See, for instance, the marvellous photograph of First World War veterans.

I could pick out several other photographs in the book that move me greatly. The hilltop view of the town in the nineteen fifties, dramatic and moody under its pall of smoke. The picture, so reminiscent of a Lowry painting, of Fred Shann pushing his bassinet loaded so highly with rags as to hide him. A picture that works so powerfully because there is no other vehicle or sign of life, against the background of starved hills. For me, the masterpiece is one of the most recent pictures. A farm auction at Height in 1982. Thirteen men and one woman, of all ages, in their drab coats and parkas against the driving sleet, huddle in a miry yard. There is no indication as to whether or not they are there to bid, or whether they are spectator-neighbours, or relatives. I think they are there to pick up whatever bits and pieces might sustain their own barely surviving existence. With hindsight, it seems that they – instinctively perhaps, and without surface consciousness of it – are witnessing a tragedy, and this seems written on every face. Strong characters all of them, sensing that this is the end of an era, hardly knowing what their future will be.

Todmorden's unique William Holt (unique not only because he was splendidly self-educated and self-enlarged, but because he embraced both a usual northern working-class radicalism and also a deeply spiritual perspective), a great autobiographer whose books should not be out of print, though a less successful novelist, used to inveigh against Todmorden's lack of pride and self-respect. "Two Nobel prize-winners came from this little town!" he used to say, "And there isn't a plaque to the one of them." (Which was true at the time.)

Some in Todmorden had an envious distaste for Billy. Despite his brave campaigning, the initiative of his travels on horseback, and his inventions even, he was regarded I think as something of a dreamer, a mere talker. But he belongs in the remarkable pantheon of Todmorden's sons … the Fielden brother who campaigned in Parliament for a reduction in working hours – "an honourable exception to his class" as Engels described him – and the Nobel Prize Winners, Cockcroft and Wilkinson. Much of what he dreamed of has occurred, and is part of Todmorden's contemporary vitality. I remember how excited he was when German speaking Ukrainians opened the first "Continental Delicatessen" in what is now the Bear Café. He was down there every day, speaking one of the several languages he knew well.

Perhaps this wonderful book of photographs will do something to help with the survival of that true pride - combined with, instead of being defeated by, the new Todmorden that Billy dreamed of and that seems now to have taken root.

Glyn Hughes

Todmorden in 1960.

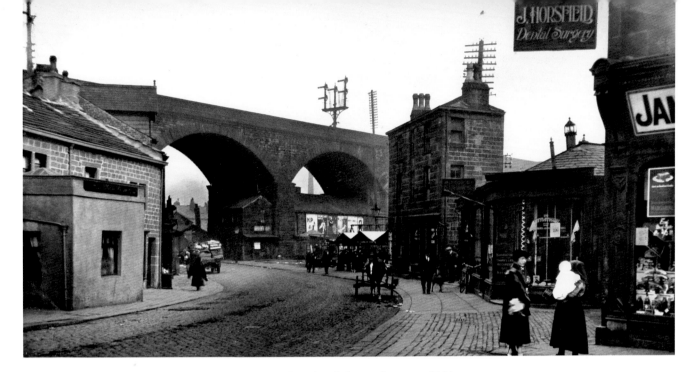

Burnley Road and the market area, 1920s.
This view shows the properties that disappeared with road widening in the 1930s. The single-storey block on the right housed three shops: Marshall's men's hairdressers, Mitton's refreshment rooms (pie and pea café) and Langstreth's butchers, at 2, 4 and 6 Burnley Road, respectively. The tall building housed a tobacconist's and sweet shop and had a room upstairs used by local businessmen as a drinking club, called The North Street Club, but more commonly, the 'Pussyfoot', after a prohibition club of that name. Another men's club, albeit with more intellectual aims, was the Merlin Club, located above Barritt's fish and chip shop underneath the arch. Members included Billy Holt, the journalist Eli Heard and the writer and artist, Edward Clapham.
The old Black Swan Inn, at left, with its tap room extension, was rebuilt by Massey's Brewery in the mid 30s.

The same view in the 1950s. Market stalls now occupy the space next to the viaduct – the site traditionally taken by the fair on its twice-yearly visits. In the early 1960s this area became the bus station and the fair was relocated to Stansfield Road. Duckworth's grocers, at the corner of Bridge Street, was part of a regional chain of grocers with six branches spread around Todmorden. The 'Emporium', owned and managed by Ruby Sutcliffe, was considered to be the town's premier fashion shop for over thirty years.

The Oddfellows Hall, Bridge Street, 1902.
There is an air of anticipation in this scene outside the Town Hall. People are milling about as if waiting for the start of an event – possibly a procession. A beggar sits by the fountain holding out his cap, while children stand by watching.
The Oddfellows Hall, then headquarters of the Todmorden Liberal Club, is festooned with flags and bunting in celebration of the impending Coronation of King Edward VII.

Workers dismantling the Taplin Memorial Fountain, 1929.
The drinking fountain, on Bridge Street, was dismantled in September 1929 after it was found to be badly corroded. The fountain was a square, cast-iron structure with a lamp on top and four water outlets with metal cups attached. It was replaced by a smaller, stone-built memorial in Centre Vale Park.
The fountain was erected in 1881 as a tribute to the Unitarian minister, Lindsay Taplin, for his leadership during the Cotton Famine and the smallpox epidemic of 1874.

Burnley Road shops, 1968.
Serda's – the name was made up from the initials of the Gledhill family – kept the two interconnected hardware shops until 1979. They also ran a taxi service from above the shop. Next door to Hartley's snack bar was the 'Carter's' Club (formerly Cattle Market Inn), a working-men's club which made no attempt to modernise, a fact that did not deter its patrons. The building was condemned by the local council in 1971 but somehow managed to escape demolition and is now the vet's. Boocock's fruit and veg business was well-established, with a stall on the outside market. The sign on the shutters read 'Say it with Flowers, Say it with Our's'.

Boots chemists, Bridge Street, c.1930. In common with many town centre shops in the 1930s, Boots stayed open until late in the evening on market days. Boots established in Todmorden in the late 1900s.

North Street, c.1905.
The building on the corner dates from the mid 19th century. Until about 1868, the whole of Todmorden's banking was done here. It was first occupied by the Manchester and Liverpool Bank who built the bank at the other end of Church Street (the present NatWest) when they left these premises. In this picture, the Yorkshire Penny Bank are in occupancy, with J O Sager's solicitors offices on the first floor. The shop with the advertising placards is Crowther's stationers and newsagents.

John Kettley signs autographs following the opening of the Tourist Information Centre, at 13 Burnley Road, 1988.
The Information Centre was one of Todmorden's success stories of the 80s, the result of a team effort by volunteers, led by architect Jack Taylor, to establish a centre where books, leaflets and information about Todmorden could be found and where bookings for shows and accommodation could be taken. The centre was additionally welcomed for the opportunity it gave to view exhibitions of art and local interest. TV weatherman, John Kettley, came back to his home town to carry out the official opening on 21st May 1988.

Roger Birch

The former Church Institute, July 1924.
The building stood at the entrance to White Hart Fold, where the first open market was held in the 1800s. When Thomas Greenlees took this picture he was well aware that the building would soon be history – the sign on the wall informs that the site was to become the Union Bank of Manchester.
The date of the building is uncertain, but an early vicarage stood on the site at one period, and around 1840, it was enlarged to three storeys. A cabinet maker's workshop and sale rooms occupied the upper floors.
In November 1884, the building was re-opened as a Church Institute – a kind of social club and rallying place for churchmen of the district. The ground floor was a reading room, the top floor a billiard room and the middle floor a 'smoke and conversation' room. The Church Institute had a short existence, however, and was wound up through lack of funds in 1899. After the First World War, the upper room was used by the Church Lads Brigade, and for a period in the 1920s, it was a practice room for Ronald Cunliffe's famous boys' choir.

The Union Bank, mid-1930s.
The bank later re-opened as Barclays (the parent company) who completely remodelled it in 1961. While rebuilding took place, the bank relocated to premises on the opposite corner – here occupied by the Yorkshire Penny Bank.

Church Street, 1889.
St Mary's Church is seen without the east chancel, added in 1896.
This early image shows the weigh-bridge – just behind the strolling hens – used for weighing wagons and their loads. The wooden hut was the office in connection with the weigh-bridge. Pasted on the hoardings are the principal notices of the day. One reads 'Wanted: workmen, farm labourers, maid servants, for America. High wages. Free farms. No rents to pay.' Another announces a 'Grand Exhibition of Art Treasures' to be opened in the Town Hall on March 11th 1889.

Construction of Birdcage Walk, 1926. The wall along Church Street was set back two or three feet to provide extra road width and a raised footpath constructed between White Hart Fold and Rise Lane. A number of graves had to be moved in the process and screens were erected temporarily to deter potential sightseers and preserve a sense of decorum. The footpath was unofficially christened 'Birdcage Walk', presumably because of the high railings, giving the birdcage effect.

Thomas Greenlees

Snowstorm, 25th February 1933. Thomas Greenlees was on hand to capture this image of a cart-horse cautiously making its way round the Town Hall.
In the background, a crowd can be seen outside the White Hart where a lorry has come to grief, blocking the way to the station.

County Bridge, Halifax Road, *c.*1965.
The fate of this three-storey block and adjoining properties was sealed in the early 60s when the County Council acquired the leases in preparation for major road redevelopment. Demolition was carried out in the spring of 1969.
The Co-op chemists and opticians, seen here, relocated to Dale Street. Other shops simply closed for good. A petition was organised to try to save the historic Grapes Inn on Church Street, but to no avail: the Grapes closed without fanfare or announcement on 8th May 1968.

Thomas Greenlees, left, with his assistant, John Taylor, outside his saddlers shop at 13 Church Street, 1910-12.

Thomas took over the saddlery and living accommodation in 1910, on the death of his father's cousin, Anthony Greenlees, with whom he had served his apprenticeship. His work making and repairing harnesses and other leather goods, together with keeping the shop, left him little time to pursue his favourite leisure occupation.

He first became involved in photography as a young man living with his parents on Der Street. To supplement his income, he would take pictures of his neighbours and their families using Spring Gardens allotments as an outdoor studio. He was meticulous in documenting his photographic activities, from date and subject to expenditure and monies received. In 1906 he helped to found the Todmorden Photographic Society with which he was closely associated throughout his lifetime, eventually becoming an honorary life-member.

The Greenlees family were well known in the town: Thomas's older brothers, Charles and Sam, ran a smithy on Der Street, while his sisters, Sarah and Alice, kept the Corner Café at Church Street for some forty years.

After Thomas's death in 1946, his youngest daughter, Haidee, single-handedly carried on the sports and saddlery business until her retirement in 1982. She was the last of five generations of her family as saddlers in Church Street.

The foundation stones of the Free Library were laid on the morning of 'Charter Day', August 22nd 1896, the day when Todmorden celebrated its newly-granted status as a borough. This historic picture – one of the first ever taken of a mass public event in Todmorden and one of the most spectacular – records the scene as the stones are lowered into place. Crowds of eager sightseers pack Neddy Bridge and the canal-side to get a glimpse of the proceedings. Among the dignitaries present is Caleb Hoyle, soon to become first Mayor of Todmorden.

The stones were laid by A G Eastwood, the Provisional Mayor, and William Jackson, president of the Todmorden Co-operative Society, the library being a gift of the co-op by way of celebrating its jubilee.

The day's events continued with a grand procession through the town, a charter banquet at the Town Hall, and to round off the celebrations, a spectacular firework display and bonfire was mounted at Longfield enabling people to see it from most parts of the town.

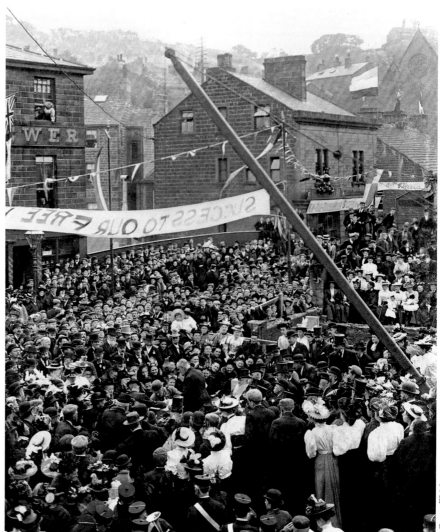

The Free Library was formally opened on 27th November 1897 by Councillor William Ormerod using a gold key presented to him by the Todmorden Co-operative Society.

This view of the reading-room around 1905 is immediately recognisable – the tables are still in use today. Gas lighting is in place (electricity was installed in 1906) and portraits of local worthies hang on the walls.

A Children's Library was launched in 1948 in the room to the left of the main entrance.

Church Street and Strand, taken from a Lilywhite Series postcard of the 1920s. The shop on the corner of Water Street, constructed over the river, had been an ironmongers since the building's origins in the 1870s. It is occupied here by Stockdale's; Beckton's followed, and from 1935 to 1972, it was King's ironmongers. The shop with the sun blind, 1 Strand, was Pilling & Elder's women's wear and drapery. This shop later became 'Johnny' Mitton's, home furnishers.

Gatley's, Water Street, 1908.
Gatley's electrical engineering business was the first of its kind in Todmorden, established in 1907 at 7 Water Street. In the early 1950s, the firm moved to larger premises at 15 Water Street (on the corner of Dale Street) where they remained until the business finally closed in 1999. Gatley's was the largest electrical contractors in the district employing at one time or another over 120 men.
In this picture, dated February 1908, the founder, Will Gatley, is pictured, left, with the foreman and two of his electricians outside the original shop.

Co-op cart horse, 1906.
Tom Smith, standing with his horse on Oxford Street, worked as a coal carter for the Tod Co-op. The horse, 'Captain', belonged to the co-op and was stabled on Oxford Street, but at weekends Tom took it to graze in a field near Shoebroad. The horse would sometimes wander down to look for him, standing in the doorway of his home at Bankside while the Unitarians were arriving at church.
The picture was taken on the morning of July 7th 1906, in preparation for what was to be the last Lifeboat Saturday event. The photographer had a special interest in his subject: he had made the saddle and harness, and later that day, it gained him a prize in the parade.

Water Street, viewed from the Town Hall in the 1940s.
On the left, the Midland Bank – built on the site of the Temperance Hotel in 1922, and (right) Horace Hartley's chemists which transferred from smaller premises at 16 Halifax Road, swapping with Mills' mens outfitters.
The Snack Bar, seen next to the parked truck, continued until the 1960s under the management of the Paolozzi family.

Staff of the Grocery department, Todmorden Co-op, Dale Street, c.1910.
Pictured from the left: Harry Mitton, Albert Crabtree, and the manager, John Bentley. The boy is unidentified. Albert Crabtree started work half-time as a grocer's assistant at the age of twelve and progressed to manager, working at various branches during his long service with the Co-op.
The window display shows a variety of bacon and ham, sauces, tea, 'Camp' coffee and other well known brands – Colman's Mustard, Quaker Oats and Bird's Custard – as well as the co-op's own 'CWS' products. A notice in the window offers 'Great Reductions on Coal and Butter'.
When the supermarket opened in 1967 this shop became the new Paint and DIY department.

'Krazy Kuts' supermarket, Dale Street, about 1970.
Todmorden's first food supermarket, erected in 1967, replaced the fire-damaged section of the old co-op building. By this time, the new owners of the Co-op and its remaining branches were the Rochdale Pioneers. The 'Krazy Kuts' offered a new style of shopping where customers could serve themselves. Competition came a year or so later when Hillard's opened the 'Lion' supermarket on Bridge Street. This picture shows pre-decimal prices advertised in the window.

The Todmorden Co-operative Stores, Dale Street, 1984.
The Drapery and Tailoring departments, at the Oxford Street end of the building, closed in July 1984 after continuous service for almost a century. Other closures followed over the next few years, and in February 93 the building was finally shut down.
The last remaining department, Electrical (re-named 'Metro'), relocated to the supermarket further along Dale Street, and was later incorporated within the new Co-op which opened on Halifax Road, on the site of the old Albion Mill. The Dale Street building was finally demolished in January 2000.

Ellis Wood and the Astorians.
This 1950s snapshot lovingly records the passing of an era. Dance halls would soon reverberate to the sound of rock and roll. Here, however, the Co-op Hall – the old Assembly Room of the Todmorden Co-op – plays host to Ellis Wood and his Astorians, the resident dance-band which played every Saturday night throughout the 50s. Indeed, the hall became known at that period as 'The Astoria Ballroom'.
The members of the band seen here are, from the left: Bob Miles (trumpet), Frank Greenwood (piano), Gerry Kirk (sax), Ellis Wood (playing clarinet), Russell Wood (drums), Frank Barker (lead alto, here playing clarinet), Kenny Potentier (bass), Harold Hirst (tenor sax) and John Butterworth (tenor sax).

Halifax Road, c.1937.
This is one of a pair of before-and-after photographs showing the effects of street lighting. In this picture, gas lamps are still in place before the change-over to sodium discharge in 1938.
The shops, from the right, are Crowther's jewellers, Mrs Bradbury's hat and gown shop, Donald Mallison's provision shop, and Smith's dyers and cleaners. From the left, are Edgar Marshall's travel agents, the Halifax Building Society, Redman's grocers, Cunliffe's mens outfitters, and Shaw's shoe shop.

Old property, Halifax Road, 1926.
This relic of earlier days disappeared under the demolisher's hammer in July 1926. The building, which stood below road level, on Meadow Lane, pre-dated its neighbours and may at one time have been a barn or provision shop on the old coaching route.
The empty shop on the left would soon become the Electricity Showroom; hitherto, it had been a second-hand furniture shop, kept by Fred Pickles, Mayor of Todmorden in 1923-4.

Julie Goodyear makes a guest appearance in Todmorden, Saturday 3rd June 1978. A gathering crowd of onlookers and fans, eager to see her 'in the flesh', greeted the soap star as she arrived for the opening of Playland Bingo, on Calder Street. Julie, alias 'Bet Lynch' from *Coronation Street*, called the first game at 11 o' clock then stayed a little while to chat to visitors and sign autographs.

Located next to the Brook Street Post Office, in what is perhaps Todmorden's most unloved building, Playland Bingo only lasted a year or two, eventually to be replaced by a fruit and veg business.

Arthur Wilcox ('Wilkie') is pictured in the doorway of his ladies fashion shop at 11 Halifax Road, 1984.

Wilkie's, 'The Bargain Hunter's Paradise', replaced Redman's grocers in the late 1960s. Famous for having possibly the world's longest retirement sale (lasting over two years), Wilkie was also well known for the interesting advertising notices he displayed in his window. Classics included the puzzling 'Plenty of Rain', advertising his stock of rainwear, and the eyebrow-raising '100 camels inside', alerting shoppers to the vast choice in camel coats on offer. Wilkie's was eventually replaced by Lady Blazers, half of the clothes shop which also took over Tony Lofthouse's children's clothes shop next door.

Looking along Rose Street, from the corner of Union Street, 1973. The Central Methodist Church is on the right.
The stone back-to-back terraces between Brook Street and Roomfield School were cleared away in stages between 1973 and 1975. Back Brook Street became, essentially, Bramsche Square. The streets in this picture – Temperance Street, Myrtle Street and Cross Street – became the Health Centre in 1985-6.
The bakery on Cross Street, centre, displayed a memorable sign in the window which read 'B. Barker. Baker'.

Omega Street, 1975.
The houses on Omega Street, as with those in neighbouring streets, lacked many of the basic amenities we now take for granted. The outside loos were still in use until the properties were vacated.
The wall on the right was the perimeter wall of Roomfield School.

The Sobriety Hall during demolition, 1975.
Opened in 1851, the Sobriety Hall, on the corner of Rose Street and Union Street, was Todmorden's first public hall. With its large, upstairs function room and several smaller rooms, the Hall played host to a variety of local organisations – sporting and religious, musical and scientific – and along with the Co-operative Hall, was a popular venue for concerts, dinners and dances.

Myrtle Street, 1973.
Jack Hammond, a weaver at Derdale, steps out for a breather while his sister, 'Dolly', chats to the neighbours.

JW Crabtree with scholars, 1905.
The hand of moral guidance can be felt in this study of boys with their headmaster and mentor, Mr Crabtree. The informality of the group, and the symbolic cricket bat, suggest this could be a school cricket team, or perhaps a recreational class. John William Crabtree (1862-1936) was head of Roomfield Junior and Half-Time School from 1893, and of Roomfield Council School from 1900, a position he held until his retirement in 1925. In addition, he served as head of Roomfield Boys' Evening School for 24 years. His great passion in life was cricket.
As a leading player with the Todmorden club he was well known in both counties, particularly in the Lancashire League. From 1885 until 1903, with the exception of three seasons when he was a Saturday pro (one season at Littleborough and two at Walsden), he was a regular member of Todmorden's first eleven, and captain for over ten years.
No doubt his performances on the cricket field made his scholars regard him with even greater admiration.

Teaching staff of Roomfield Boys School in 1920.
From the left, back row: Peter Gannon, Agnes Nuttall, Mary Seel, Arthur Cecil Dawson. Middle row: Maggie Mitchell, John William Crabtree (headmaster), Annie Hartley. Front: Katie Pilling and Gertrude Pickles. All the women were unmarried at the time.
Mixed classes were introduced when Roomfield became a Senior and Junior School in 1931. John Bentley became head of the Senior School, while Mary Hannah Farrar, previously Girls' School headmistress, became head of the Junior School.

Roomfield School, viewed from Hazlewood Street in 1977. The Infants entrance and playground are on the right.

Constructed in 1877 as a single-storey building, the school was enlarged three times before 1900 to take account of the rise in child population, particularly within the school's central catchment area. The building contained separate Boys', Girls' and Infants' schools and, from 1893, an 'Organised Science School'. Housed on the upper floor of the building, this higher grade school was officially designated a Secondary school in 1901.

In 1914, a child welfare clinic was established in the Roomfield Street extension, with a full-time medical officer and nurse who treated children's minor ailments. A dental clinic was added four years later. (These facilities were replaced by the Abraham Ormerod Medical Centre in 1938.)

Following educational reorganisation in 1946, all senior schools were amalgamated at Roomfield, the leaving age having risen to fifteen. With over 700 pupils, the school was clearly inadequate for modern day needs and scholars were obliged to travel to Lumbutts, Cornholme and other 'satellite' schools to complete their education. In 1957, the Secondary Modern School transferred to new, purpose-built premises at Scaitcliffe.

When dry rot was discovered in 1975, Calderdale officials declared the building 'unsafe', and the following year, the Infants School removed to Stile – the old Open Air School. Demolition began in April 1977.

Many prominent Todmordians received their education at Roomfield during the school's 100 years' existence, and none more celebrated than Sir John Cockcroft. For a few years, he and William Holt were contemporaries under J W Crabtree and when Cockcroft went 'upstairs' to the Secondary School, Holt became a half-timer, and left altogether at thirteen to become a weaver.

The Mayor of Todmorden, Dr Stella Brown, presents Coronation mugs to Roomfield pupils in May 1953.

Shaw House, 1970s.
Shaw House was one of four shops between Cross Street and the York Street Chapel – the block stood roughly where the Myrtle Street entrance is today. It was named after a Mr Shaw, a director of Mons Mill, who opened it as a pie shop and cafe in the 1930s. During World War II, Shaw House was one of five British Restaurants in Todmorden serving cheap, wholesome meals such as Woolton Pie. After the war it became an antique shop, first kept by Marion Fielden and then by John Chadwick. The 'Shaw House' fascia was retained by the various tenants, the last being Jeffrey Knowles who ran it as a model shop in the 1970s. The block was pulled down in 1979.
Next door to Shaw House in this picture is Halstead's confectioners and tobacconists. The shop on the left had been Jackson's drapers.

Roomfield House, c.1900
The gate and perimeter wall are all that remain of this substantial house and grounds, the former home of Caleb Hoyle and family, which stood on the site of the present Roomfield Court sheltered housing.
After Caleb Hoyle died in 1915, his widow and their four daughters moved to Southport. The house then passed to the youngest son, Joshua Hoyle, who lived there with his family until 1925. Soon afterwards, in accordance with the wishes of his sister, Alice, he presented the house to the Todmorden Christian Science Society and it became a church for the members of that faith. The building stood empty for many years before it was demolished in the 1960s.

Laying of electricity cables, Halifax Road, 1904.
Todmorden Corporation received Royal Assent in 1901 to lay distributing mains along the three main roads of the town centre. A site for the generating station was chosen at Millwood, and in 1904, plans submitted by the Electrical Engineer were proceeded with.
The supply was switched on on 13th October 1905.
Initially, electricity was only suitable for lighting purposes, but by 1915 it was being used extensively for mill-driving. In 1926 a showroom was opened at 10 Halifax Road to demonstrate the amenities of electricity in the home and promote the hire-purchase of cookers.

Church Lads Brigade procession, 1920s. The brigade, headed by their officer-in-charge, Crossley Atkinson, march along Halifax Road past the entrance to Canal Street and Lower George Street.
The single storey building, originally 'The Black Cat' billiard hall, of 1911, later became part of John Bentley & Sons, printers.

Employees of Lord Brothers' Canal Street Works are pictured at the entrance to their Lower George Street workshop, 1905-10. The apprentices are seated at the front.
In its heyday, Lord Bros was one of Lancashire's leading manufacturers of cotton spinning and preparatory machinery, producing many of their own patent improved designs. By the 1900s, a major part of the business was devoted to export, with machinery shipped to India, China, Japan and Brazil.
In 1920, the company was bought out by the Manchester firm, Brooks & Doxey. Nine years later the Canal Street Works was shut down and manufacturing transferred to Manchester: it was easier to access transport routes from Manchester than it was from Todmorden. 250 jobs were lost and it was the end of an era for the town.

Lord Bros moulders, c.1925.
The foundry at Stackhills Road (later Kinghorn's engineering works) produced ironwork for the various carding, scutching, doubling and ring spinning machinery made by the firm.
Ralph Rowland took this picture of his workmates unaware that he would be unemployed within a few years. As an apprentice moulder in the 1890s, one of his jobs was to collect horse-droppings for mixing with the sand as a binder. When the circus came he walked his wheelbarrow all the way up to the Holme and collected elephant droppings instead, but they were unsuitable.

Williamson's provision shop at 83 Halifax Road, c.1930.
Will Williamson, on the left, with his partner, Crossley Leah, sold corn, proven and other animal feed, as well as farm implements, bread, cigarettes, and a variety of domestic items. Although they owned a wagon, they made deliveries to the local farms by horse and cart until the late 1940s. The shop was next to the Hippodrome Cinema.

Hubert Ashworth, at his shop at 133 Halifax Road, September 1986. Hubert is pictured shortly before his retirement, having run the business for 37 years. The pharmacy was transferred to the more central position in Bridge Street, (previously Boots' chemists) where it was carried on by his daughter and son-in-law under the name Ashworth's.
The Halifax Road shop subsequently became Hussain Brothers' grocery.

'Procession of Witness', 8th April 1977. Organised by the Todmorden Council of Churches, the march was a familiar sight in the town on Good Friday. This iconic image captures Walsden churchwarden, John Lord, and an unidentified cross-bearer making their way up Halifax Road, oblivious to an overtaking Mini.

Martin Parr / Magnum photos

William Simpson ('Old Sinbad'), shirt manufacturer, local Rechabite official, Band of Hope leader, temperance reformer and prominent Liberal is pictured in the orchard in front of his home at Hallroyd Cottages, about 1912. In his book, *I Haven't Unpacked*, William Holt describes his first employer, 'Old Sinbad', who took him on as a half-timer in 1909: "The proprietor was a short, stout, fussy old man with a round, untrimmed grey beard and a pair of steel-rimmed spectacles".
William Simpson's factory, called the Bee Hive Works, was at the bottom end of Dale Street. He also had a factory on Salford which burnt down at the end of the first world war.

Derdale and surrounding area, July 1930.
The industrial landscape takes on a clearly defined pattern in this bird's-eye view, taken while the mills were shut down for the annual holidays. The mills and factories – as they were in 1930 – are identified as follows. From the left, on either side of Stackhills Road, the former Lord Bros foundry and machine shops; Sandbach's weaving shed (Hope Street Mill); Croft Mill; Anchor Mill; Stott's weaving shed (Der Street Mill), Jeremiah Jackson's engineering works (with the small chimney, centre); Hoyle's spinning mill and weaving sheds (Derdale Mill), which became John Cockcroft & Sons Ltd in 1936. The 3-storey spinning mill was sub-let to T Hill & Co, screen textile printers.
On the other side of Key Sike Lane is Sandholme Mill (occupied by the British Picker Co), the Spring Gardens allotment area, and far right, the Sandholme Ironworks. Stansfield Corn Mill is prominent at Hallroyd, top centre.

Sandholme Ironworks, late 1890s.
This faded image is the only known photograph of the Sandholme ironworks, founded in 1893 by Thomas Lord. The picture was almost certainly commissioned, and records the entire workforce outside the foundry which was accessed via Commercial Street. The factory, which produced castings for textile machinery, was sited next to the canal for convenience of transport – boats brought in pig iron and took away the finished goods to Manchester.
The firm, which became known as the Sandholme Iron Company in 1903, has seen three changes of ownership since then. The present owners, Weir Warman, are part of an international company supplying pumps to the mining industry.

The Rochdale Canal boat 'Daisy', moored at the Sandholme wharf, about 1910.
The men appear to be unloading grain for Sutcliffe's corn mill. Cargoes of flour would be transported back to Manchester by the same method. In its time, the canal conveyed the bulk of Todmorden's manufacturing output, from machinery to cotton goods.
The old size-house of Derdale Mill, seen here, remained standing until 2004.

George Sunderland, with 'Jock', outside the stables on Commercial Street, May Day, 1950.

George Sunderland (1897-1964) loved horses and spent his working life as a carter delivering coal for James Mitchell Ltd, coal merchants, on Stansfield Road. He routinely delivered to six factories in the town – Joint Stock, Coupe's and West's in the Stansfield Road area, Sandbach's and Stott's in Halifax Road, and Crescent in Rochdale Road – and made house calls in the afternoons. George worked with 'Jock', the last of the Mitchell draught horses, up to 1956 when the horse was put out to grass at Stoodley. On May Days, he always followed the traditional custom of special grooming and plaiting ribbons into the horse's tail and mane. Tragically, George was killed in a road accident just two years after his retirement in 1962.

In this picture, Betty Ashworth is peering round her doorway, left, while Cissie Moss shouts to her neighbour, "Hey, come and have a look at this!".

Swimming at Derdale, 1900s.
Mill dams, reservoirs, and particularly the canal, became magnets for young men and boys during spells of hot weather. It is not known whether the youths pictured here are boat crew or local lads cooling off after work.

Part-time auxiliary firemen line up for a photograph in the Fire Station yard at Waterside, 1940. The picture was taken to mark the arrival of the new pumps. The Officer in Charge, Mr Cooper, is first from the left.
Set up in 1939, the Auxiliary Fire Service was made up of local working men who signed up as part of the national Civil Defence programme. They were provided with training and equipped to deal with fires in wartime situations. Crews of six rotated on nights while the regular Fire Brigade was off duty.
In 1941, most of the men pictured here were 'called up' for National Service, but were retained as part of the new National Fire Service.

Todmorden 'War Weapons' Week, Sunday 2nd May, 1941.
Crowds of local people and school children gather on the market ground to listen to the opening speeches by Commander Stephen King-Hall, of the Ministry of Aircraft Production, and Flight-Lieut Malcolm McCorquodale. The captured Messerschmitt 109 was on display throughout the week of the campaign, which raised a final total of £400,341 from a population of 20,349.

'Salute the Soldier' Week, May 1944.
In 1944, Todmorden, along with other towns and cities across Britain, took part in the nation's 'Salute the Soldier' campaign. The object locally was to raise £200,000 to equip and maintain a base hospital for one year.

The week of events was officially opened on Saturday 13th May by Lady Louis Mountbatten and proved to be an enormous success. A huge thermometer-like indicator was placed outside the Town Hall, and each evening at 7 o'clock, an indicator-raising ceremony took place.

The news that the target had been surpassed by £60,000 was announced on the Friday evening by Rev. Brinley Davies – seen here with the Mayor, Harold Taylor, the Mayoress, and a detachment of the Girls Training Corps. The raising of the indicator was accompanied, to the delight of the crowds, by the hanging of the devilish 'Squander Bug'.

No.1 Platoon, Todmorden 'A' Company of the 21st Battalion Home Guard, are pictured at Blackshaw Head during manoeuvres, 1942.

The platoon sergeant, Crossley Leah, is first from the right on the front row. Originally called the Local Defence Volunteers, the Home Guard was an army of civilians formed in 1940 to help protect and police the country. The volunteers were usually men who were too old to serve in the regular army, or worked in 'reserved occupations'.

The first headquarters of the Home Guard was on Rochdale Road, in a building opposite the Conservative Club, later at the British Legion club in White Hart Fold. Manoeuvres took place on the hilltops every Sunday, with Todmorden alternately attacking and defending against Hebden Bridge. Blank cartridges, fireworks and flour bombs were used as ammunition.

Fifteen year-old Mary Whitham cleans the family's footwear at 29 Tennyson Avenue, Todmorden, 1945.

This image first appeared in *Picture Post* in June 1945 as part of a 3-page article by the author and broadcaster William Holt. Entitled 'Bringing Up a Very Big Family', the article featured the Whitham family, of Tennyson Avenue, with whom Holt was familiar.

Willie and Elizabeth Whitham, who had just celebrated their twenty-sixth wedding anniversary, were parents of sixteen children - eight boys and eight girls. In their previous home, they had rented two houses side by side and made them into one by knocking through. Now, with four of the boys in the Forces and the eldest daughter living with relatives, there were just thirteen at home in this two-up two-down council house.

The article dealt with the logistics of managing and providing for such a large family. Writing on the eve of a general election, Holt makes the point that, with new social reforms on the way – school meals, home help, family allowances and comprehensive healthcare – large families could thrive without the kind of problems that the Whithams have had to face.

*Footnote:* this image later appeared in a promotion for Cherry Blossom shoe polish.

Mrs Whitham studies the family's ration books to work out what she can buy. Ration books became familiar to every citizen during the war. The books contained food coupons that the shopkeeper would remove before issuing the goods. For certain non-essential items, such as canned foods, a points system was introduced: everyone was allowed 16 points a month, later raised to 20, to spend at whatever shop that had the goods.
Mrs Whitham had 312 points to spend.

Jack Highley's cloggers hut behind the market hall was a familiar fixture until the 1980s.

Professor John Cockcroft greets his former teachers, 5th October 1946. On that day, the town honoured one of its most illustrious sons by making him a Freeman of the Borough, the highest recognition that the council had the power to confer.

During the ceremony at the Town Hall, Professor Cockcroft spoke of his early upbringing and the influences on his life and paid tribute to his former teachers at the Todmorden Secondary School. Later, he had the opportunity to meet four of his old mentors. He is pictured here with Miss Johnson, Senior Mistress, and Miss Lord (centre), who taught him applied art and languages. Also present were the former headmaster and physics teacher, Mr Ernest Farrar, and Mr Luke Sutcliffe who taught him mathematics. John Cockcroft was among the first intake of the pupils who transferred from Roomfield to the new school at Ferney Lee in 1912.

Local schoolgirl Bernice Webb presents a bouquet to Mrs Cockcroft during the Freedom ceremony.
Elizabeth Eunice Crabtree, of Stansfield Hall, (known to her friends and family as 'Neecie') was married to John Douglas Cockcroft, of Birks House, Walsden, in 1925.

Sir Geoffrey Wilkinson (1921-96): a portrait of the physicist and research chemist, taken while he was professor of Inorganic Chemistry at Imperial College, London.

Born and educated in Todmorden, Geoffrey Wilkinson was widely regarded as one of the chief influences in the field of 20th century chemistry and during his career received many national and international honours. In 1965 he was elected a Fellow of the Royal Society, he received the Nobel Prize, jointly with Professor Ernst Otto Fischer in 1973, and in 1976, was knighted for his contribution to Chemistry.

Always proud of his Todmorden roots, Sir Geoffrey was delighted when he was granted honorary citizenship of the town in 1990.

Geoff Love is presented to the Queen before a Royal Filmharmonic performance at the Royal Albert Hall, late 1970s.

On several occasions throughout the 70s, Todmorden born Geoff Love was invited to arrange and guest-conduct for the Filmharmonic in concerts celebrating the works of film music composers Michel Legrand, Nino Rota and John Williams, and the films of Walt Disney. The 'Filmharmonic' has been a regular feature in the calendar of the Royal Philharmonic Orchestra since 1970.

Ridgefoot, Burnley Road, 1905.
Todmorden is reminiscent of a frontier town in this early photograph. The road surface is typically unpleasant following a recent rainfall. Improvements were to come about in 1912 when street paving was introduced.
The buildings here remained relatively unchanged until the bus station development in the late 1980s. The clogger's hut in the centre survived virtually intact. The building on the right, more recently a butchers, was at that time a pie-and-pea café, kept by William Sutcliffe ('Billy Fatlamb') and his wife. Posters on the wall announce a concert of the Musical Society and, taking place on March 12th 1905, the Sunday School Anniversary of Bridge Street Methodist Church, with a sermon by Dr Brook. The ground at the rear of the buildings became the Cattle Market in 1902.
Previously, the monthly cattle fairs were held on the market ground itself.

Paolozzi's, Burnley Road, 1973.
Open seven days a week, from 9 am to 8.30 pm, Paolozzi's ice cream kiosk was 'a little goldmine', enjoying quick sales of sweets, tobacco, soft drinks and ice cream. It was especially popular with cinema-goers in the years following the war when the Olympia showed films twice-nightly.
Rita Paolozzi ran the shop for 37 years before retiring in the mid 1980s. Her family came to Todmorden in 1947, a year later purchasing the Neil's Ice Cream business.
The cloggers hut next to Paolozzi's was kept by Fred Pinnington who started shoe repairing after the war. For a period in the 70s there was a resurgence of interest in traditional clogs and Fred was kept busy making them to order. He retired in 1986.

Geoffrey Baron

Will Gibson's studio, Victoria Road, 1979.
The asbestos-clad timber building was opened as a portrait studio in 1904 by Albert Wood, a former teacher of music. The studio then passed to Hebden Bridge photographer Crossley Westerman who, with his daughter Sara, ran it during and after the First World War. Will Gibson acquired the building in the late 1930s, and after serving as a photographer with the RAF, established a portrait and wedding business here. Throughout the 1950s - 1970s, many of the Mayors of Todmorden sat for their official portraits in the studio, and the window provided a showcase for Will's most recent work. When he retired in December 1979, the hut was taken over by Neil Arnold who ran it for a few years as 'The Victoria Road Studio'. It has since been a storage facility.
In this picture, Martin Crowther and his sons are seen with Kenneth Priestley. The large building in the background is the Employment Exchange.

Stuttard's wagon, on Blind Lane, 7th July 1906.
Carrying a display of cotton warps, the wagon is photographed after taking part in the 'Lifeboat Saturday' parade, a mile-long procession of floats and vehicles representing most of the town's trades and industries. The firm of Matthew Stuttard's ran Knowlwood Bottom Mill at that time.
The building in the background, at far right, is the Victoria Road Primitive Methodist Church, re-opened in 1929 as the St John's Ambulance Hall.

Residents of Victoria Road venture out to see for themselves the devastation left by the flood. Judging by the debris in the street, the worst is now over, but no doubt Burnley Road is still submerged. Flooding was a recurrent problem in this area: whenever the culvert under Victoria Road became obstructed the pressure of water would lift the flag-stones, resulting in flooding in the low-lying streets around Patmos and Wellington Road.

Wellington Road, viewed from the Garden Street end, is completely inundated in this early 1900s picture. Residents can be seen peering out of bedroom windows while a couple observe from the shelter of their umbrella.

Burnley Road in flood, 1931. The heavy rains during the early morning of November 4th caused chaos to factories in the Stansfield Road area which were forced to shut down due to the extent of the flooding. The water also caused complications at the site of the new Olympia cinema, seen here, where piledriving was in progress.

Workers on the Calder College construction site group together for a picture in 1953-4. Peter Staroszczuk (front row, second from left) came to Todmorden from the Ukraine in 1949 and went to work initially for Cockcroft's, at Birks Mill; however he did not like working in the mill and when offered a job on the college site he accepted. He was the last person to leave when the building work was completed in 1955.

Jubilee Day, Monday, 6th May 1935. Three thousand children from the borough's sixteen schools took part in celebrations for the Royal Silver Jubilee of King George V.
Viewed from a third floor window on Burnley Road, the children can be seen marching in procession to Centre Vale where they they are to take part in a gala of inter-school sports, football and netball matches, followed in the evening by a spectacular firework display.
Before the day, each schoolchild was presented with a souvenir mug, a bank passbook with a deposit of one shilling, and a copy of the Jubilee supplement of The Manchester Guardian.
The children are marching past the forecourt of the new Olympia Cinema, on the left, and the houses where the Community College stands today.

Frances Barsby and her sister, Priscilla, at their milliners and children's wear shop at 26 Burnley Road in 1904.
At this time, there were nine milliners flourishing in Todmorden. Frances Barsby was a dressmaker by trade and lived with her sister and their parents in the flat above the shop. Three years after this picture was taken, Frances was taken ill with tuberculosis, and died at the age of 27. Priscilla carried on running the shop until 1926, when her life also ended prematurely.

Dr William Currie, pictured outside his home, 'Riverside', about 1912.

Dr Currie was one of four doctors practicing in the Burnley Road area at this time. He was unmarried and lived with his sister and their three domestic staff.

Riverside was a semi-detached property until 1923, when the house was made into one for Dr Vincent Southwell and his family. It was used as a day nursery during the Second World War, and in 1954, became the police station.

The 60th year of Queen Victoria's reign was commemorated by a gift to the Parish Church of eleven bells. The peal of bells was presented by Miss Hannah Howarth, of Brocklyn House, in memory of her late brothers and sisters.

This photograph records the arrival of the first eight bells on 7th June 1897. Among those present are the Vicar of Todmorden, Rev Canon Russell, MA (fourth from left) and the curate, Rev A S Roberts (second from right). Leaning on the bell, left, is the photographer John Binns (of Lord & Binns' Studio, Wellington Road), who, presumably, has just set the camera exposure before taking his place within the ensemble. When Christ Church closed in 1992 the bells were transferred to Towcester, in Northamptonshire.

The main hall of the National School, about 1905. The view here is towards Burnley Road – the windows on the left look on to the cricket field.

For many years, the hall was a common area housing two or three classes. Later, moveable partitions were introduced allowing discrete teaching areas. The upper school children and teachers would gather here each morning for assembly before going off to their respective classrooms.

The school, at this time, catered for around 340 children, aged five to fourteen, of which there were nine classes – a 'Babies' class, two Infants classes and six Standard Elementary classes. Std VI – the 'top class', with up to fifty pupils – was taught by Mr Hesselgreaves whose desk can be seen on the right. The pupils sat at iron-framed bench desks, evidently without back-rests. Illumination, when daylight was inadequate, was provided by the overhead gas mantles.

On the platform, separated by screens, were two more classes (Std II and Std III) and behind this, facing Burnley Road, the classroom of Std I. On the first floor, overlooking the boys' playground, was the 'Parish Room' – used exclusively for Sunday school and church-related activities.

The National School, 1905.
This commemorative picture of boys lined up in the yard was taken in April 1905 at the retirement of John Turner, who had been headmaster for 38 years. Assistant master George Hesselgreaves (standing with his back to the wall) was promoted and served as headmaster until his retirement in 1932.

Todmorden Schoolboys cricket team, 1949.
From the left: Malcolm Heywood, Donald Haughton, Keith Marshall, Colin Anker, Trevor Lumb, Peter Brownbridge, Richard Sykes, Harry Hazeltine, Maurice Greenwood, Roger Moss and Dennis Widdup.
The team was managed by local teachers Alan Watson and Arthur Sykes and played in the Roch Valley League.

This picture tells its own story. Cricket club life-member, Leslie Forrester, and committee man, Clifford Greenwood, gloomily survey the scene on the morning of 5th August 1982: what was yesterday a lush, green sward was now a filthy lake. Following the deluge on Wednesday afternoon, children took the opportunity to swim in the 5 ft of water covering the cricket field, but as the flood subsided, a thick layer of mud was left behind. Almost immediately, an army of volunteers, led by the chairman, set to work shoveling, hosing and pumping, and by the following week the ground was virtually back to normal.

The Cotton Queen of Lancashire judges the Children's Dog Classes at the Todmorden Agricultural Show, 13th June 1931.

Frances Lockett, a nineteen-year-old millworker from Hyde, was England's first Cotton Queen who spent a year travelling the country promoting cotton at public events. Her visit to Todmorden in 1931 was one of the highlights of the 'Cattle Show'. She pictured here with some of the young exhibitors.

The little boy with the white socks is Bernard Shaw; next to him, holding the terrier, is George Ashworth, and the boy at near right is Arthur Robinson.

There was an amusing incident as she judged the children's dogs. "What is your name", she asked one of the young exhibitors. "George Bernard Shaw" came the surprising answer. Everyone smiled, because George Bernard Shaw was a little schoolboy from Cornholme.

'Britannia' and her attendants are pictured at the opening of 'Wings for Victory' Week, Centre Vale Park, on Saturday 5th June 1943.

The colourful Empire Pageant, which followed the opening ceremony, was presented by the Unitarian Church and pupils of music teacher, Sylvia Forbes, and dancing teacher, Hilda Holt. 'Britannia' was performed by Alice Hollinrake, 'Peace' by Alice Greenwood (left), and 'Prosperity' by Mary Sutcliffe. Ten year-old John Wild (right) played 'John Bull'.

Todmorden 'Wings for Victory' Week raised a total of £265,936 for the war effort.

Enoch Horsfall

First World War veterans remember their comrades, late 1960s.
Every year, on the Sunday nearest the 5th May, the remaining veterans of the First World War would meet at the War Memorial to commemorate their old comrades. The service was organised by the Todmorden Detachment of the 1/6 Lancashire Fusiliers Old Comrades Association, of which former fusilier George Scriven was the long-serving secretary. During the service, a wreath of red roses and yellow tulips (the regimental colours) was laid on the war memorial bearing the inscription "In memory of absent comrades. From the 1/6 Lancashire Fusiliers Old Comrades Association". A wreath of poppies was laid by a member of the Todmorden British Legion, and the service closed with the traditional recitation of Laurence Binyon's lines "They shall not grow old as we that are left grow old".
Present in this picture are, from the left: Harry Grindrod, Bill Smith (representing the British Legion), Harold Pilling, Jim Holt, unidentified, George Scriven. Billy Barker, Charlie Baldwin, John Willie Barker, Eric Lord (trumpeter), and Billy Fielden.
A year or two later, Eric Lord arrived at the usual time and date to find he was the only one there. He sounded 'The Last Post' alone before leaving.

Veterans of Todmorden Bowling Club assemble for a group photograph in 1996.

The opening of the bowling greens at Centre Vale, 8th June 1915.
Events taking place in the wider world overshadowed the opening of the much-awaited bowling greens. The first of two greens was formally opened by the president of the British Crowned Bowling Association, Mr J W Coombs. Seen here 'testing' the green is the Mayor of Todmorden, Robert Jackson, with Alderman William Ormerod in support. The gentleman with the top hat, at far right, is Alderman Banks. The man with his hands linked, fourth from right, is Crossley Sutcliffe.

Carr Laithe, 1890s.
Carr Laithe was a small farm on the Centre Vale estate owned, until 1912, by a descendant of the Fielden family. It was from here, in the 1850s, that the young John Fielden (son of 'Honest John') courted and later married the farmer's daughter, Ruth Stansfield. In its picturesque setting on Lover's Walk, Carr Laithe was a popular subject with photographers and many views were reproduced as picture postcards. The last tenants of the farm moved out in the late 1930s and the building remained standing for a further seven or eight years.

Incident on Lovers Walk, 1940s.
News & Advertiser reporter, Sam Tonkiss, and a young policewoman see the humorous side of a potential disaster: a driver, Geoffrey Knowles, took the short route down Buckley Wood when he failed to negotiate the bend at the top. His girlfriend was with him at the time.

The Recreation Ground, Ferney Lee, c.1904.
The rec' was situated on the lower side of the railway, where the Calderdale elderly persons' home is today. Opened in 1902, it was to all intents and purposes a small park with flower beds, walk-ways and benches, with a separate playground for children at Lower Ferney Lee. Concerts were given there by the Todmorden Old Brass Band and the whole area was looked after by a uniformed caretaker who rang a bell to indicate closing time.
With the opening of Centre Vale Park in 1912, the Recreation Ground became superfluous, and in 1920, the first Open Air School was erected on the site.

Todmorden in the 50s.
Smoke-abatement campaigner, Harry Stansfield, took this, and a series of pictures in the 1950s to show the effects of smoke pollution. He complained bitterly that the Town Council took no notice, despite the fact that the Clean Air Act of 1956 had given them powers to create 'smokeless zones'. In 1961, the Council finally recognised that household chimneys accounted for more smoke pollution than did the mills and duly declared a section of Burnley Road to Lineholme as the first Smokeless Zone.
The view here is from Royd causeway, looking over Park Road. The large house on the left is 'Glenroyd', built in 1890 for Sugden Sutcliffe, and used as a nunnery from the late 1920s.

A typical haymaking scene at Royd Farm, 1902. West View and Hollins can be seen in the distance, left.

Friends and relatives would often help out at haymaking time, which usually fell at the beginning of July. Only one person in the group can be identified: the boy third from left is eleven-year-old Rufus Dawson, whose uncle, Tom Dawson, farmed at Royd at this time. Rufus became a pharmacist and worked at Timothy White's and Taylor's, in Water Street.

The Mount, 1905-10.
A terrace of six houses on the hillside behind Stansfield Hall, 'The Mount' was built in 1900 utilising stone from an adjacent quarry. For many years, the terrace was commonly referred to as 'Klondike', a reflection of local humour: people at the time thought the builder, Jim Firth, had "struck gold" with The Mount, presumably because his raw materials were so handy.

The Meadowbottom Treat, 1928-30. Before the days of television and holidays abroad, families got together to provide their own entertainments within their local neighbourhoods.

Typical of these was the Meadowbottom 'treat', organised by the mothers of Meadowbottom during the inter-war years. The treat would consist of games, races and refreshments (usually school buns and tea), at a suitable location – in this case, East Whirlaw Farm. Before the day, the children would go around the neighbourhood soliciting small donations towards the costs.

Seen on the far right, in this picture, is Mrs Macriel, known to one and all as 'Old Mother Mac'. A legendary character in Meadowbottom, Mrs Macriel was always on hand; whenever there was a birth, death or similar emergency: the call would go out "Send for Mother Mac!"

Stansfield Hall Lodge, c.1900. George Brammah is pictured with members of his family outside their home, the old lodge, or gate-house, which stood at the entrance to Stansfield Hall Drive (near the present Fountain Inn).

When Stansfield Hall was a private estate, gates were hung across the road at this point from two stone pillars. On top of the pillars were coping stones around which were carvings of leaves representing every type of tree planted on the estate.

The lodge was demolished in 1964.

Ruth Bramley, Holebottom, 1976.
Like many local hill farmers, Ruth Bramley (1906-86) and her husband, Will, managed to sustain a living from dairy farming. The small herd they kept at Holebottom Farm provided enough milk for their daily customer round with any surplus left at the depot at Fielden Square. In this picture, Ruth delivers milk to a neighbour's while taking her cows to graze in a pasture near Wickenberry, only a stone's throw from where she lived as a child.

Holebottom Mill, c.1910.
An early water-powered spinning mill, Holebottom Mill fell into disuse until Joseph Shuttleworth took it over and adapted it into a steam laundry in 1895. The washing was transported to the mill by a horse-drawn van until 1916 when the firm acquired an early motor van. However, the vehicle was not capable of climbing the hill fully-loaded and the driver often had to rely on the young 'lads' of Meadowbottom to tow and push the van up to the mill.
The end came a year or two later when, on 1st February 1918, the mill was destroyed by fire. 'Oakhill' was built from the ruins, a home for Philip Hoyle and family, complete with tennis courts where the mill dam had once been.

J O Sager and son, at Adamroyd, 1904.
When this picture was taken, only a handful of people owned a motor car. The solicitor John O Sager, seen here with his son Maurice, lived at Holly House but his car could not get up the steep Meadowbottom Road so he kept it at Adamroyd, on Stansfield Hall Road.
The three-storey building at top left is West View.

Stansfield Hall Station.
'Stansfield Hall for Todmorden' was opened in 1869 so that Yorkshire to Blackpool trains did not forget Todmorden completely. Although somewhat inconvenient for the town centre, the station was popular with locals travelling to Burnley and opened up holiday destinations on the Fylde coast. In the 1930s there were typically seven trains a day from the station with an extra one on Saturdays. Despite local opposition, the station was closed in July 1944.
This picture is thought to have been taken in the late 1880s. The coach house and stables of Adamroyd can be seen in the background, and on the far hillside, Royd, as it was before the main house was enlarged.

Herbert Hardaker

Train smash, Stansfield Hall Station, 1904.
The accident occurred on 5th December, involving a heavily freighted goods train of seventy wagons en route to Wakefield. As the train descended the gradient between Copy Pit and Portsmouth, the couplings broke and the train divided into two parts. When they realised what had happened, the drivers of the two engines, now with ten wagons in tow, put on speed to try to get clear but were forced to stop at Stansfield Hall when they found the signals against them. The rear portion smashed into them, damaging the station platforms and one of the stone piers of the iron footbridge. Several wagons tumbled down the embankment and into the grounds of Adamroyd, where a summer house was destroyed.

Hallroyd Crossing, 1890s.
The level crossing at Hallroyd was removed for safety purposes in 1896 and replaced with a road bridge some 75 metres west of the old crossing.

Herbert Hardaker

Leonard Helliwell, Todmorden Station, 1910.
Leonard Helliwell (1891-1975) left school at thirteen to work for the Lancashire & Yorkshire Railway Company. He was a goods guard at Todmorden for most of his working life, eventually retiring as goods inspector at Bury. He is pictured with the parcels delivery van at the entrance to the goods yard on Ridge Road.

John Ramsbottom (1814-1897) rose from modest beginnings in Todmorden to become one of the foremost railway engineers of the 19th century.
His grandfather had built the first steam-powered factory in the town in 1804 and it was here that John Ramsbottom learnt the basics as far as mechanical engineering was concerned. By 1857 he was head of the Crewe Works, at that time one of the largest locomotive workshops in the world. His many inventions and improvements for the standardisation of locomotives and parts brought about huge benefits in productivity. Later he helped select the site and design the Horwich works of the Lancashire & Yorkshire Railway Company, and in this was so successful he was asked to become a director, which he remained until shortly before his death. In July 2003, a plaque was unveiled at Todmorden Station in recognition of his life and achievements.

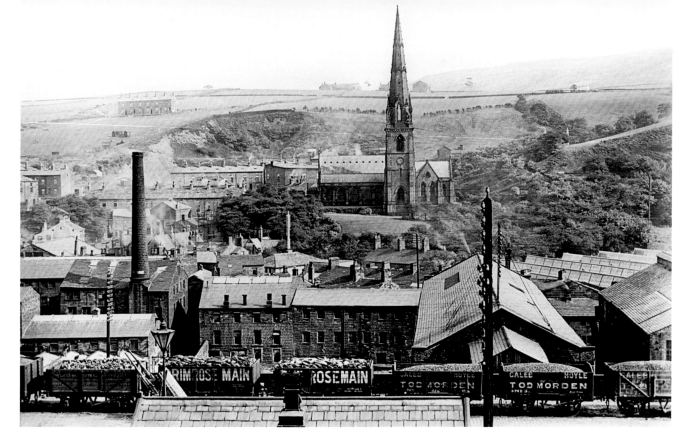

View over the sidings at Todmorden West, 1905-10.
The infill behind the 'Great Wall' of 1881 provided space for sidings extending all the way to Dobroyd. Here, coal wagons exclusively for the use of Caleb Hoyle's can be clearly seen.
As well as affording a clear view of the Unitarian Church, this picture takes in part of the industrial complex at Salford. The chimney at left belongs to Astin & Barker's 'Victoria Ironworks', in the centre is Whitehead's sheet metal engineering works, and on the right, the Canal Company warehouse. At far right is the 'new' shed of Fielden Bros' Waterside Mill.

Dobroyd Road, about 1910.
The crossing keeper's hut and cottage can be seen, centre, and the roof of Fielden Bros' warehouse on the right. Dobroyd Road would have seen considerable activity during the era of railway construction. Nearby Lob Quarry provided stone for the Todmorden railway viaduct and many local buildings. In later years, the road was improved and maintained by the Fieldens as their main access to Dobroyd Castle.

The Fielden Monument, c.1903.
The statue of John Fielden MP was moved from its original position outside the Town Hall to Fielden Square in 1890. Encircled within protective railings, the Monument – as it was then known – became the centrepiece of Fielden Square. It was moved once again, in 1939, to Centre Vale Park.
The statue was commissioned from the artist John Foley in 1861 with the proceeds of a public subscription throughout Lancashire. When completed, it was placed in storage until a suitable site could be found, then, on 3rd April 1875, it was formally unveiled at the opening of the Town Hall.
Here the statue is set against the Unitarian Chapel (later Sunday School) which John Fielden founded in 1824, however, the stars of this picture are the two urchins sat on the side.

Wellfield Terrace, 1901.
The houses at Wellfield Terrace were a combination of back-to-back upper dwellings and one-room dwellings on the ground. Built in 1851-2 by the Lumbutts Club, they were sold to the trustees of the Independent Order of Oddfellows in 1884. At the time of this photograph, they were known as 'Club Houses'.
The picture is one of a series taken to support a court case brought by the Oddfellows who complained of a shortage of water to the houses from Goshen Lodge, a small dam some 200 metres away. A legal battle ensued which the Oddfellows lost.
Wellfield Terrace was pulled down in 1977.

Bank Street, c.1901.
Standing at the doorway of 15 Bank Street is Richard Stansfield, with his wife, Sarah, and four daughters from a previous marriage – Ellen (holding the baby), Mary, Patience and Sarah. When this picture was taken, Richard was working as a mechanic fitter for Jeremiah Jackson's, millwright engineers at Der Street Mill. His son James was also a mechanic fitter for the firm, having started out as an apprentice loom-maker for Fielden Bros. His grandsons, Harry and Richard, would also make their careers with 'Jer's', Harry eventually becoming managing director in 1946. Richard Stansfield died in 1908 aged 65. Bank Street (Goshen Terrace at the front) was demolished in the late 60s.

King Street, Fielden Square, c.1914.
In the 19th century, Longfield Road was more commonly known as 'Hanging Ditch', the name gradually becoming lost in the mist of time. King Street was the conduit into Longfield Road but disappeared from the map when the old properties next to the Golden Lion were taken down.
This photograph was taken by the Unitarian minister, Arthur W Fox, from his top-floor flat above the Conservative Club.

Chew's Garage, Rochdale Road, early 1930s.
Jack Chew is pictured with his 24-seater coach outside the garage at Fielden Square. The coach was available for general hire and regularly took fans to the All-in Wrestling at Royton on Sunday afternoons (passengers were charged 1/- for the return trip). Around this time, Geoff Love was working at the garage as an apprentice motor mechanic, his first job after leaving school. Over the garage was Cunliffe's printers, and on the top floor, accessed from a stairway at the rear, the 'Empire' billiard hall. The ground floor, before Chew's took over, had been a printing works – the *Todmorden Advertiser* was printed here, a rival to the weekly *Todmorden & Hebden Bridge District News* printed by Waddington's a few doors away.

This picture, from around 1930, records a new acquisition for Maurice Wilson's, the fruit, corn and vegetable suppliers who operated from Canal Yard, next to the Golden Lion. The founder, Maurice Wilson, originated from Pontefract where the firm grew much of their own produce at farms they owned. At the height of their business, they had five wagons delivering to over 100 shops a day, including pubs, chip shops, co-ops, Duckworth's, and many independent grocers. Two chip shops – Brook Street and Victoria Road – regularly ordered one ton of potatoes each per week. The wagons were also used for haulage and house removals, and at holiday times, fitted with coach bodies for trips to Blackpool.

The business was sold at auction in Manchester in 1960 and later bought by one of Maurice Wilson's former employees, 'Bunny' Rothwell, who ran it for several years under his own name.

Canal Yard, in the early 1970s.
The cavernous structure, next to the Golden Lion, had been used in the late 19th and early 20th century as stabling for the horses of the Todmorden Carriage Company and the town's Fire Brigade. Later, it became a depot for Maurice Wilson's, the fruit & veg suppliers.
From the 1960s until the mid 80s it was a scrap-yard, first run by Ellis Schofield, then by Roy Dunlevy and his operative, Alma Knight. For a few years, prior to demolition in the mid 1990s, it was a motor repair shop.
In 2002-4, the site – now known as 'Fielden Wharf' – was transformed into a mooring and service facility for canal barges.

This row of derelict shops on Rochdale Road was awaiting demolition in 1980.
In 2002, the transformation of the area was complete with the creation of a green 'gateway' site to Todmorden.
The second property from the end, with the bay window, was opened as a Board of Trade Labour Exchange in 1911 and became the British Legion Club in 1923. The middle shop was a branch of Duckworth's grocers.

Postmen line up for a photograph outside the Post Office, about 1912. Only two can be identified – Sam Greenwood, first from left, and Fred Thomas, fourth from left.

Opened in July 1904, the Crown Post Office was built next to the existing telephone exchange on Rochdale Road. Many people thought the location inconvenient, and by the 1920s, the building was becoming inadequate. In 1924, a decision was made to transfer the Post Office to Todmorden Hall. The old building, which is still in use (presently as a furniture upholsterers) subsequently became the Ceylon Billiard Hall and also housed a ladies' hairdressers ('Louie De Vere Green's'). From the 1940s-60s it was a laundry ('The Snow White Laundry').

Cheapside, Rochdale Road, 1973.
This row of shops was cleared away in the late 1970s allowing a better access into the Salford industrial estate. The remaining half of the block now forms Waterside Lodge. The Lord Nelson Inn (the 'Admiral Lord Nelson' of 1795) closed in 1975, as did the newsagents next door.
The middle shop, during the first half of the century, was a pawnbrokers run by a Mrs Briggs and her daughter.

Herbert Greenwood sold pies from a wheelbarrow after suffering injuries while working at Derdale Mill. He is seen here at Waterside in 1910. He died only a few years later, in 1916, while still quite a young man.

The paving of Rochdale Road, 1911. The increasing presence of motor transport in the late 1900s was in part responsible for the disintegration of the road surface, particularly in wet weather. In 1910, the Corporation embarked on a programme of street improvements including the paving of the main approach roads with granite setts. The first tender was let to local contractor Benjamin Lumb for the length between Millwood and the Town Hall. The second tender, for the length between Gauxholme and Ewood Lane, was let to Riley Bros & Hartley.

In this picture, work is progressing at Crescent (near the present entrance to Morrison's). One of Caleb Hoyle's wagons can be seen carrying empty skips to their mill at Walsden.

Close encounters at Waterside, 30th March 1971.
The identified flying object is the Futuro house, manufactured and marketed by Waterside Plastics Ltd. Designed in Finland for use as a holiday home, the plastic house was on its way to a temporary site outside the Abraham Ormerod Medical Centre, where it would be the information centre for the borough's 75th Anniversary celebrations. The Futuro house aroused national and international interest but was destined to be a commercial flop – only two or three were sold in this country. Furthermore, the oil crisis of 1973 tripled the price of oil making production costs too high to be profitable. This particular model was exported to South Africa along with the manufacturing licence and equipment for further production.

Unitarian 'charladies', 1988.
Members of the church congregation give the interior a spring-clean in preparation for an Open Day.
They are, from the left: Annie Sutcliffe, Brenda Brook, Minnie Ormerod, Barbara Dugdale, Annie Redman, Marjorie Whitaker and Alice Stansfield. The Unitarian Church closed for religious services in the mid 80s due to dwindling membership and the ever-increasing cost of heating and maintenance. The Grade I listed building was saved from further deterioration by the Historic Chapels Trust, which now owns and manages the church and burial ground.

Wedding party at Laneside House, 1908.
This group contained the cream of Todmorden society. Tom Lord, of Hallfield, was married to Elizabeth Barker, of Laneside House, on April 23rd 1908. The ceremony at the Parish Church was performed by Canon Russell (seen here, fourth from the right, at the rear). After the wedding, the bride and groom and their families returned to Laneside for this commemorative photograph and refreshments.
Tom Lord, standing just behind, and to the left of the bride, was the founder and principal of the Sandholme Ironworks, and John Barker, father of the bride, was the elder partner of William Barker & Sons, of Wadsworth Mill.

Fred Shann negotiating Rochdale Road, 1973.
A familiar sight around town until the 1980s, Fred Shann pushed his pram from street to street collecting rags and unwanted clothing. When he had a full load he would take it one of the local scrap-yards for recycling.
Fred started rag collecting when he came to Todmorden after the war. He tried other jobs, briefly, but preferred being 'self-employed' and carried on scrap collecting until he retired.

Todmorden's first ambulance, c.1902. The ambulance and crew are seen in the mortuary yard at Waterside, in what appears to be a staged photograph to show off the new van, delivered to the Corporation in May 1902.
The ambulance was strictly for accidents and emergencies and could be called out only by a doctor. It was kept at the Fire Station where there was telephone communication and a horse available at all times. Accident victims and fatalities were brought to the mortuary where the bodies were washed and laid out by Mrs Cryer, who lived at nearby Bar Street. A legend in her own lifetime, Lizzie Cryer carried out her duties for 58 years, retiring at the age of 91.

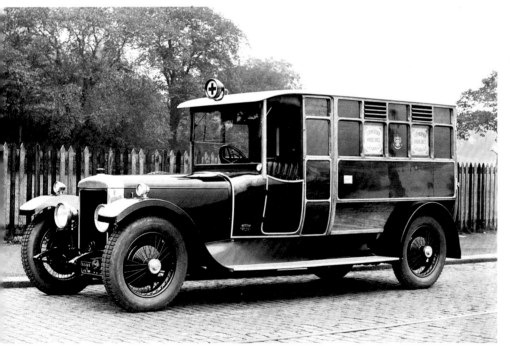

The new Daimler ambulance, presented to Todmorden Corporation in 1925 by Joshua H Hoyle, of Roomfield House. Joshua Hoyle was one of the town's most prominent benefactors, giving generously to many good causes. The Daimler was the second motor ambulance he gave to the town, replacing a Rolls Royce he presented in 1920. The youngest son of Caleb Hoyle, first Mayor of Todmorden, Joshua was the head of J H Hoyle Ltd, Hollins Mill, Walsden, the largest employer in the village at that time. He died in 1929, aged 46, when tragically he failed to survive an anaesthetic while in the dentist's chair.

St Mary's Church of England School, Oak Street, 1973.

St Mary's was the first purpose-built school for the children of Shade and locality. Opened in January 1868, St Mary's Mission School – as it was first called – provided for both day and Sunday scholars. The front of the building, shown here, faced Wadsworth Mill, with a rear entrance on Bar Street. The Church was responsible for the school's upkeep and for all educational matters until 1901 when the school was handed over to the local School Board. After Shade Council School was opened in 1904, St Mary's continued to be the Sunday school and hosted a variety of community and church-related events – concerts, tea parties and socials.

In September 1975, the building was demolished, along with the rest of Oak Street, as part of an area improvement scheme.

Geoffrey Baron

Shade, viewed here in 1973, was one of the first areas to benefit from improvement schemes. The building lower right, together with the old Bridge End Co-op, were demolished to provide car parking and greenery. The white-painted property was a fish and chip shop.

Roger Birch

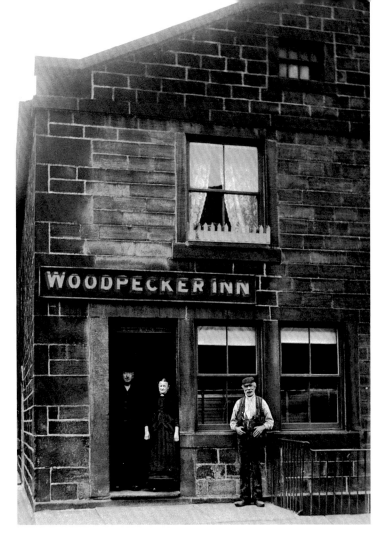

The Woodpecker Inn, Shade.
Dating from the mid 19th century, the pub was extended in the late 1960s to include the adjoining property.
This view, from around 1895-1900, shows the proprietress, Sally Hollinrake, standing in the doorway.

This picture from the 1890s shows the butchers shop next to the Woodpecker, with members of the Greenwood family who kept it at this time.
The boy is holding a pole-axe, typically used by butchers. Part of the slaughter-house can be seen, far right, on Little Holme Street.
The shop remained a butchers until the 1950s and then re-opened for a short period as a fishmongers. Eventually the property was acquired by Wilson's Brewery.

The Steele family, of Shade, 1907. There are many photographs recording Todmorden's early buses but this picture is rather unusual in that it features several members of the same family. The conductor, Albert Steele, centre, is pictured with his father, Charles Steele, in front of the family's newsagents' shop at Waterloo, Shade. His mother, Isabella, is standing outside the shop and his sister can be seen peering around the shop doorway.

The picture is thought to have been taken in the first few weeks of 1907, shortly after the bus – one of two Crichley-Norris motor buses made to order for Todmorden Corporation – made its maiden run from the Town Hall on New Years Day 1907.

Charles Steele, then aged 58, was well known in the Shade area. As well as a shop-owner, he worked as a warehouseman for the Bridge End Co-op which had its headquarters directly opposite the family shop, and was also secretary of the co-op's Education Committee. Albert Steele later gave up his job on the buses to become sub-postmaster at Shade, a position previously held by his younger brother, Frank.

The Bridge End Co-op, as it appeared in the 1930s, following amalgamation with the Walsden Co-operative Society. The grocery department is on the left, the drapery and shoe department on the right. The doorway at the top of the steps, right, led to the general office where, twice a year, regular customers could collect their 'divi' – a form of cashback amounting to two or three pence in the pound.

On the top floor of the building were the Assembly Rooms – one large room and several ante-rooms – used for dances, tea parties, soireés and meetings of the Society.

The Bridge End Co-op ceased trading in 1966, by that time having been subsumed within the Co-operative Retail Society. The building was occupied for several years by light industry before demolition in 1975.

Shops at Gauxholme, 1973.
The garage and filling station, established in 1914 by W H Midgley, was a thriving business until the late 60s. After Midgleys packed in, the garage lay empty for several years until David Macdonald took it over and restored it in 1976.
White's, next door, was a small independent bakery run by Dora White and her daughter, Jean.
Shade Post Office had been a drapers prior to 1921 when the shop's owner at the time, Enoch Whitehead, was appointed sub-postmaster in succession to the late Albert Steele.
The shop on the right was a hardware and spare-parts shop in connection with the garage.

Pilling's fruit delivery van, outside their shop at 262 Rochdale Road, 1930s.
In a highly competitive market (grocers were in abundance) Everett Pilling took to the streets to augment his sales. After inheriting the fruit and veg business from his father in 1932, he acquired the Croft three-wheeler which he ran for about eight years. One of his specialities was ready-peeled potatoes.
The shop, directly opposite the gates to Shade School, had two windows – one displaying fruit and vegetables and the other, sweets and confectionery, making it a popular destination for children on leaving the Baths.

Shade, viewed from Knowlwood Road, 1962.

Shade was in a transitional period when this picture was taken. The Vernon Place flats, left, erected in 1954, replaced the old terraced houses at Vernon Street, Ivy Street, Cable Street and Lewis Street. Further clearance of derelict properties was carried out along Rochdale Road. Shade Mill, which had been Fielden Holt's picker works since around 1900, awaited demolition, the subject of a compulsory purchase order.

The little shop would be the last to go, clearing the way for the Charles Place development. The shop was always known in the locality as 'Little Bark's', after its long-time proprietor, Barker Greenwood.

The Rochdale Canal at Shade, c.1910.
A canal driver, accompanied by a local schoolboy, leads his horse along the towpath at Shade, the boat 'Charlotte' having just negotiated the Gauxholme Lower Lock.

Drivers were employed by the Canal Company and worked in stages of about ten miles, a relief and fresh horse being ready for the boat at each stage.

Stabling for fourteen boat-horses was provided at the Gauxholme Wharf.

Knowlwood and Copperashouse area, c.1904.
Canal, road and railway interweave in this fascinating panorama from Watty Lane. The Gauxholme viaduct cuts across the site of an early 19th century mill dam – used as a scrap-yard during the 1940s. On the far side of the viaduct is Knowlwood Bottom Mill, operated at that time by Stuttard's as a warp sizing and cotton weaving concern. The flue from the mill's boilers was carried underneath the main road to the chimney standing alongside Little Knowl Terrace.

The Navigation Inn, Gauxholme, 1912.
The history of the 'Navi' is inextricably linked with that of the Rochdale Canal which it pre-dates by several years. The inn – originally the 'Hare and Hounds' – was altered and renamed following the construction of the canal. A third storey was added, providing a large clubroom over the rest of the building.
Situated by the canal-side off Bacup Road, the inn would have been a haven for travellers, mill-workers, and bargees resting over the weekend. When the canal as a means of transport went into decline so too did the fortunes of the pub which appears to have closed quietly in the 1930s.
The man standing in the doorway is Billy Cheetham, the landlord at the time.

The entrance to Gauxholme Fold from Bacup Road, *c*.1955.
The houses to the right of the enclosure were named Fustian Place (originally Tub Street) and were back-to-back with those on Gauxholme Fold.
The corrugated roof, right, was that of Midgley's vehicle repair garage, a pre-fabricated building which was erected on the site of the old Black Bull Inn.
At the time of this photograph, Albert and Ivy Young ran the corner shop.

Gauxholme, *c*.1904.
Gauxholme Fold, in the centre, was one of the oldest settlements in the district. This view from Naze takes in Pexwood Road, left, the Gauxholme canal wharf, lower left, and Midgelden Clough, far right, which passes under the canal to conjoin with Walsden Water. The disused mill dam, below right, became the site of 'Naze View'. The tall chimney, centre, is that of Dancroft Mill, while the chimney to the right belongs to the former corn mill, destroyed by fire in 1899.

Thomas Greenlees

Motorcycle trials, Naze Road, 1925. On Sunday, June 7th 1925, some 3,000 people descended on the normally quiet and secluded area of Watty, in Bacup Road, to witness an interesting motor-cycle event.
The Liverpool Motor Club had chosen the seemingly inaccessible Naze Road for hill-climbing trials. The hill was regarded as one of the most difficult in the country, the gradient 1 in 3 in some places. It had been climbed once or twice in the past by local motorcycle enthusiast, Maurice Greenwood. Despite several stop starts, after getting stuck in gulley-stones, most of the riders made it to the top and continued along the moor-edge before returning to Bacup Road via Walton's picker works. A Rhode car (seen here) driven by the club's captain also made the ascent, but not without help from spectators.

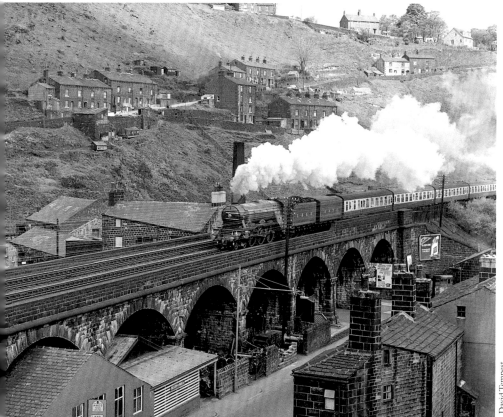

David Tempest

*The Flying Scotsman* crossing the Gauxholme viaduct on 1st June 1969. The famous locomotive was brought out of preservation for a trainspotters 'special' to Newcastle, via Bradford, Halifax and Carlisle. The train's brief appearance in the Calder Valley was recorded by dozens of photographers, including David Tempest who took this shot from the rear of the Spinners Rest pub on Knowlwood Road.

The Chaffer sisters, Watty Terrace, Bacup Road, 1984.
The sisters were all born in the Shade area and attended Shade Council School, subsequently learning to become weavers in the local mills. They are, from the left, Renée, Marian, Winnie, Nellie, Gladys and (seated) Edith. They were photographed for a feature in *Woman* magazine in February 1984.

Robert Stansfield ('Bob o' th' Stones') leads the singing of *The Farmer's Boy* at the Todmorden Farmers' Annual Ball, January 1956.
The ball, then in its 36th year, was the annual get-together of local farmers and their families. The highlight of the evening came around midnight when, with the dance-floor crowded, Robert Stansfield would take up the microphone to lead the ceremonial singing of *The Farmer's Boy*.
He said he first sang it in 1927 "because it seemed appropriate".
Supporting him on the platform at the Town Hall are the Mayor, Herbert Hardy, Ernest Trafford (far right), and Edgar Hirst, farmers' union representative (second from right).
Robert Stansfield farmed at Stones Grange from 1908 until his death in 1969.

Members of the Todmorden Photographic Society visit Townley Hall, 1954. Summer outings to Lancashire and the Dales were regular events in the calendar of the Photographic Society often commemorated with a group photo.

While it is not possible to name everyone here, the front row, from the left, are: Peter Lever, Colin Lever, John Elliman, Rudy Holzapfel, Lynn Lever, Richard Holt, the next two unidentified, and Ann Barker. In the second tier are Clara and Jack Lever, Fred Elliman, Will Kerr, Robert Cunliffe and Arthur Barker. At the rear are Richard Howarth, Geoff Kerr and Cecil Nutter.

Thirteen-year-old Peter Lever discovered his vocation when he joined Todmorden Cricket Club in 1954. He went on to play for two full seasons with the club, in 1958 and 1959, before signing for Lancashire in 1960. Ten years later, he made his test debut on a tour of Australia where he took thirteen wickets helping England regain the ashes. He played test cricket on seventeen occasions.

Peter's older brother, Colin, also became a county cricketer, playing for Buckinghamshire from 1962, and for Minor Counties in 1965. From 1968 to 1976 he was pro for Heywood, in the Central Lancashire League.

Rudy Holzapfel came to Todmorden in unusual circumstances. As a German prisoner-of-war, he was conscripted onto road-building in the Bacup area where he met his future wife. He joined Todmorden Photographic Society in 1949 and enjoyed considerable success in the annual exhibitions. Throughout the 60s and 70s he freelanced for the local paper while, for his day job, he was the chief photographic technician at Walsden Printing Company.

Members of the Todmorden Orchestra grouped in front of Ewood Hall, 1915-16. The newly-founded orchestra filled a gap in the musical life of the town when the Todmorden Musical Society, the town's premier musical organisation for 45 years, disbanded in 1914.

On 8th August 1915, about ten musicians met to consider forming an orchestra. There were several further meetings, then, on 3rd October 1915, in the presence of fifteen members, it was decided to call the group 'The Todmorden Orchestra'. The membership fee was 1/- with a weekly subscription of 2d. The Brass Band Room – then located above King's bakehouse on Harley Street – was engaged for Sunday morning rehearsals, the first being for a concert in aid of War Funds.

Pictured here are, from the left, front row: Charles Clegg, Sam Pavis, Tom Sutcliffe, John Wadsworth, Herbert Jackson, Walter Mitchell (Conductor), John Bentley, Barker Ackroyd, Elsie Mitchell, Harry Horsfall and Albert Starkie. Middle and back row: Ernest Playford, Harold Laycock, Wright Sutcliffe, Walter Warburton, Raymond Law, Greenwood Shuttleworth, Jim Swindells, Jacob Maden, Fred Helliwell, Arnold Nuttall, Herbert Greenwood, Will Lumb, Joe Woodhead, Wilfred Kingsbury, Jesse Stockwell, Alfred Johnson and John Ackroyd.

All were amateur musicians, working mainly in the local cotton industry and allied trades: Walter Mitchell was a warehouseman at Sandbach's. Oboe player, 'Greeny' Shuttleworth, was a shuttlemaker at Crossley's. John Wadsworth was killed in the First World War.

Dr Eric Crichton Grey in his Walsden surgery, 1976.
Dr Grey was one of the old school of family doctors who would turn out for calls 24 hours a day and seven days a week. Until his death at the age of 80, he continued to care for over 1,000 patients in Todmorden, Walsden, Littleborough and further afield. From his surgery on Rochdale Road he also ran his own pharmacy where he mixed all his own prescriptions for patients.
Born in Dublin in 1900, Dr Grey qualified as a physician and surgeon in 1924. He worked as a GP in Wales, Harrow, and at a London hospital before returning to Dublin where he again worked as a GP, and followed his favourite hobby of horse breeding and racing. During his years in Dublin he owned around ten racehorses. Dr Grey started his practice in Walsden in 1954, succeeding the late Dr Macgregor. Soon afterwards he began to breed pointer dogs which he entered in many of the country's top shows. Local people best remember him for his relaxed and informal manner – he would often drop by to see his patients while out walking his dogs.

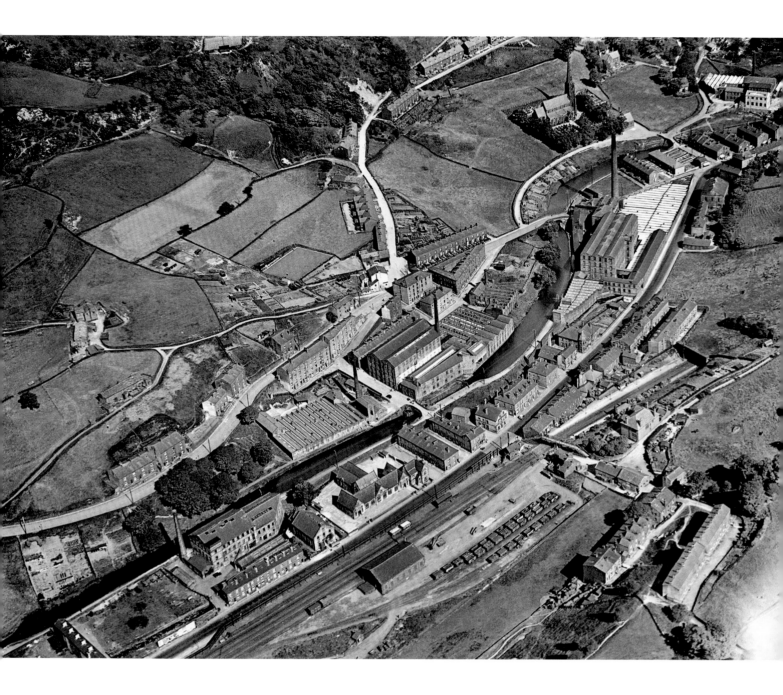

Walsden from the air, July 1930.
This unique perspective allows us to see the topography in a way not possible from the ground.
Bridging the canal, in the centre of the picture, is Alma Street, leading to Hollins Road and Henshaw Road, top centre. Church Walk is clearly defined at top right, while Walsden Station footbridge is visible at lower right. The mills are positioned on either side of the Rochdale Canal – from bottom left to top right – Lacy Mill, Hollins Bottom, Alma, Hollins, and Birks Mill.

Birkshall Toll Bar ('Birks Bar') at St Peter's Gate, was built as a toll house in 1825 for the Todmorden Turnpike Trust. Prior to 1876 – the year the Turnpike Trust expired – tolls had to be paid at various stages along the turnpike for the privilege of using the maintained and more direct routes. The toll bars were manned day and night and displayed a list of tolls for the various types of transport. Mail coaches were exempted. In 1825, the turnpike was extended along the valley from here, at Inchfield Bottom, to Bridge End, Shade. The old road went via Hollins Road, Top o'th Hill, Knowlwood, and Butcher Hill. In 1901, when this picture was taken, the former toll bar was a butchers shop kept by Young Lord who lived on the premises with his wife and two children. During the 1920s and 30s it was a ladies and gents outfitters.

The re-opening of Walsden Station, 10th September 1990.
Crowds turned out to see the new railway station declared officially open after being closed for 29 years.
The people of Walsden – glad that they were once again 'on the railway map' – crammed on to the platforms and footbridge to witness the arrival of the first train following the opening ceremony.
The new station brought back memories for many people in the village. Fred Fielden, aged 86, a former Mayor of Todmorden and a railway worker himself for 24 years, was at the ceremony with the last ticket to be used at Walsden before it closed on August 6th 1961.

Members of the Walsden School horticultural class pictured with their teacher, Mr Walter Swain, July 1912.

The class was started in 1912 by Mr Swain, headmaster of Shade Council School. The two-year course consisted of 25 lessons during the winter months, followed by practical instruction during the summer. For a fee of 2s. 6d (12p), the students were provided with the land, tools, manure and seeds, and were allowed to keep the resulting produce. Each student had a plot of land 10 metres x 5 metres in the garden which was adjacent to the church school on Birks Lane. With 72 individual plots, the garden was the largest school garden in Yorkshire.

Mr Swain said that, in view of the number of hours spent, the class did not pay financially, but it paid indirectly in providing a healthful, educative exercise, and encouraged a love of nature.

The boy standing fourth from the left is Eric W Cockcroft, second eldest of the brothers who would later play a prominent role in the town's affairs.

Reuben Crowther and his wife, Susey, are pictured outside their grocery and confectionery at 754 Rochdale Road, Bottoms, late 1890s.
The sign in the window reads 'Home Made Bread. Fresh Tea Cakes'. The Crowthers also sold their own home-made potted meat. The row of cottages still stands today, opposite the Gordon Rigg Garden Centre.

Road repairing at Bottoms, c.1896. Steam road-rollers were generally in use until the 1950s. This particular machine was the first one to be used in Todmorden. It was made by the firm of Aveling & Porter and delivered to the Local Board in 1882 at a cost of £463. For many years, it was the only one of its kind in the district and was regularly hired-out to neighbouring authorities. The full-time driver was Tom Dugdale (seen here) who was engaged in 1888 to work the roller, at £1. 4s. a week. He held the job for 25 years.

View over Walsden cricket field, around 1960.
Gordon Rigg's market garden is still in its infancy alongside Winterbutlee Mill – then part of the Bottoms Mill enterprise.
The twin chimneys are those of Bottoms Mill and Jubilee Mill. Bottoms – running 132 looms, as well mule-spinning – was the last mill in the district to carry on cotton and textile production, finally closing in 1997.
Jubilee Mill, founded and built by the Pioneer Mill Company in 1901, has been used for various purposes since the mill ceased cotton spinning during the depression of the 30s – notably as a for cocoa works for Rowntree's of York, during the war years.
Today, both mills are part of the flourishing Garden Centre business.

Walsden Carnival processing past the Butcher's Arms, Bottoms, 18th August 1956.
Persistent drizzle throughout the day failed to dampen the spirits of carnival supporters and onlookers – seen here waving on the the occupants of John Mamwell's butchers truck.
This was the sixth Walsden Carnival organised by the Walsden Cricket Club.

A view from the 1920s, showing the Strines area of Walsden.
The buildings remain today although the former tannery, at bottom left, is scheduled for redevelopment. Re-planting of trees has taken place in recent years on the upper hillside, the trees in this picture felled during the second world war.
The view looks over Ramsden Wood Road, towards Holly Bank, with the turretted roof, centre, and Walsden cricket ground at far right. The open area in front of Maple Street, right, used as allotments and hen-pens until the late 1950s, was developed for industry by the Walsden Printing Company.
Strines tannery, which closed in the 1950s, prepared raw buffalo hides for the production of pickers, for use in cotton weaving. A building in the tan-yard was utilised as a tripe works until 2002.

Rochdale Road, near Lanebottom. This picture was taken in February 1924 before a road-widening scheme came into effect.
A compulsory purchase order was obtained to demolish the properties on the roadside, including Deanroyd Mill, seen in the background.

Lanebottom, 1918-20.
This outlying Walsden village centred around its Wesleyan Methodist Chapel, seen left. Built in 1818, and enlarged in 1875, the chapel was too large ultimately for the community it served, and closed in the 1960s, the site redeveloped for housing.
Behind the chapel is Lanebottom, or Bottomley Fold, and to the right, the ventilator shaft marking the entrance to Summit Tunnel.
The building in the distance, near Stonehouse bridge, is a branch of the Walsden Co-op with adjacent reading-rooms. The building was taken down in the mid 1920s when the co-op opened a branch more centrally in Lanebottom.

Walsden United football team are pictured on their home turf at Bellholme after winning the Calder Valley Shield in 1924. The club played in the Todmorden & District League.
For many years, Bellholme was derelict land littered with scrap vehicles, but it is once more a sports area, complete with parking and changing facilities.

Knowlwood United football team, pictured during the 1923-24 season. They are, from the left, standing: J Green, I Stansfield, R Barker, G Heap, H Fielden (captain), A Dawson. Front row: I Mitchell, T Judson, L Crabtree, W Mitchell, W Fielden and W Gibson. The team were semi-finalists in the Halifax Charity Cup in 1923. Knowlwood played their home matches on 'The Rough', an inclined stretch of ground off Lumbutts Road, near Swineshead Farm. The ground was also used periodically for rugby matches.

Todmorden's first team, after winning the Worsley Cup in 1954.
Photographed on the cricket ground at Centre Vale, the team are, from the left, back row: Donald Haughton, Brian Fielden, Jimmy Moncrieff, James Burke (Pro), Colin Sunderland, John Ingham. Front: Kenneth Walker, Frank Saul, Harold Dawson and Jack Hazeltine. The eleventh man, not present, was Malcolm Heywood who was on National Service at the time and had to return to camp.
That year, the club went on to win the coveted 'double' – the Worsley Cup *and* the Lancashire League Trophy.

Members of the Hollins Tennis Club relax around the pavilion at The Grove, 1904. Essentially a sport for the middle classes, lawn tennis was first introduced in Todmorden in 1881 when a club was formed at the Hollins Inn, Walsden. The game was played on a level area above Henshaw Wood. In 1890, the club moved to The Grove, near Stansfield Hall, but retained the name 'Hollins'.

Winners of the Hebden Bridge & District 'B' League trophy, the team are photographed at The Grove in August 1953.
From the left, back row: Derek Crabtree, Jack Taylor, Harold Hurst, Donald Whitehead. Front row: Jennifer Ashworth, Sylvia Forbes, Dennis Forbes (Captain), Jenny Cockcroft and Pat Greenwood.

Hilda Turner, *c.*1930
The word 'teenager' had not been invented when Hilda Turner posed for this photograph. Born in 1912, Hilda was the youngest in a family of eight children. After leaving school she worked as a clerk for the borough council and later married Jack ('Our Jack') Sutcliffe, who became managing director of Whitehead & Sons, sheet metal engineers.

The Richmond Street Kids, 1952. Eunice Crossley took this snap of her sons, Rodney and Kevin, outside their home at 12 Richmond Street. The cowboy outfits were Christmas presents from their aunt and uncle.
In 1953, the Crossleys went to live in the Town Hall after Eunice's husband, Charlie, was appointed Town Hall caretaker and Mayor's Attendant.

Cleanliness Day at the Open Air School, 1937.
The 'war' against dirt is enacted by pupils at Stile. Seated at the front are Tom Shore and Gladys Booth. Dennis Clegg, on the right, is holding the banner.

Bath-time at the Open Air School, 1953.
Cleanliness, health and nutrition came high on the agenda at the Open Air School. In this picture, teaching assistant Dorothy Townend checks the weight of six-year-old Malcolm Maudsley, while Peter Abraham looks on, and Trevor Wilkinson takes his turn in the shower.

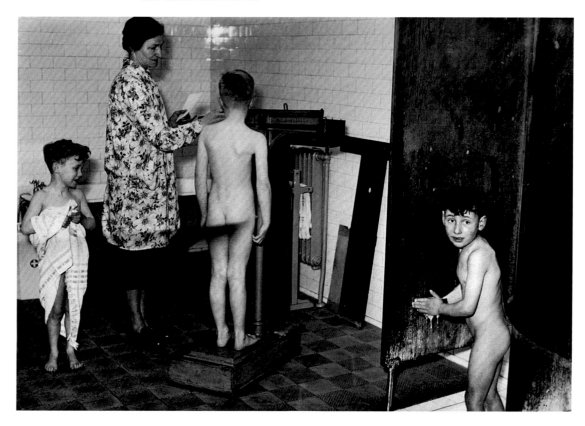

Sanger's Circus on the Holme, c.1901. Once a year, the Holme played host to Lord George Sanger's circus which would pitch camp for two nights, giving just two performances before moving on to the next town.

In this picture, elephants and other circus animals can be seen grazing on the railway embankment while a passenger train steams past. Ashenhurst Road passes under the railway and branches off to Cowhurst and Mark Lane, left, before continuing on to Ashenhurst, top right.

One of the popular side shows of the circus was the 'Darktown Fire Brigade' consisting entirely of dark-skinned people. A matchwood house would be built then set on fire, and the Fire Brigade would 'put it out'.

The circus's final visit to Todmorden came in September 1905.

Fire engine trials at Hare Mill, 1914. Local officials and visitors from neighbouring towns met at the Fire Station on 3rd October 1914 to witness the arrival of the first motor fire engine for the town, made by Merryweather's of London.

They followed the engine in a special bus to Hare Mill, where the powerful Hatfield pump was put through a number of tests. Afterwards, the engine made a trial run to Portsmouth, then to Callis Bridge, and on to Walsden for a deep lift from the canal at Hollins Bridge. In its vermilion-painted livery, the new fire engine was fitted with a 4-cylinder petrol-driven motor capable of delivering speeds of up to 40mph. Pictured outside the engine-house at Hare Mill are the Mayor, Alderman Robert Jackson (right), Councillor Fred Pickes, Chairman of the Watch Committee, and a representative from Merryweather.

Mons Mill, 1948.
This unusual view from the railway embankment shows the Lodge, left, with its distinctive green dome, used at this period as a nursery for the workers' children, and the boiler house, centre, with coal stocks in the foreground.
The chimney is seen at its full height in 1948 when the mill was working at capacity. The top of the chimney was lowered by some thirty feet in the 1970s, and razed completely in 1986, along with the engine-house. The mill was demolished in 2000.
Built from red brick, 'Hare' Mill was the work of Oldham architects, Stott & Sons, who in their day were responsible for some twenty percent of the mills in Lancashire. The south gable, shown here, was finished in unfaced brick, anticipating a future extension.

Mrs Parfitt watches a beaming frame at Mons Mill, 1949.
Operations at Mons Mill involved every process from the preparation of raw cotton to the production of spun weft. Women made up the greater part of the workforce apart from in mule-spinning, which was traditionally a male job.
The top three floors of the mill were given over to mule-spinning with twelve pairs of mules on each floor. Ring-spinning was a much smaller operation, confined to the ground floor.
In the 1930s Mons Mill was taken over by the Lancashire Cotton Corporation and sold, in 1965, to Courtauld's who closed the mill in 1969. Two years later, it was reopened by Ward & Goldstone, makers of electrical wiring harnesses for motor vehicles, later Volex Wiring Systems.

Scaitcliffe School, about 1960.
Todmorden County Secondary Modern School was opened in May 1957, pupils attending for the first time in August. Comprehensive education was introduced in Todmorden in 1979 and the school was amalgamated with Todmorden Grammar School to form Todmorden High School. With over 1,000 students, the new system had to operate on a split site for several years and a familiar sight was that of buses shuttling pupils to and fro between schools at break times.

Newton Green, 1905-10.
The entrance to Ashenhust Road is on the immediate right, the present shop and red-brick terrace built around 1919. Prominent in the background, at Cross Lee Gate, is Dean & Howarth's tannery and picker works.
The river wall, left, was set back some 10 metres in 1931 to enable a major road-widening scheme.

Scaitcliffe Corn Mill, c.1904.
This early water-powered mill, run by the Jennings family, was one of several independent corn mills in the town in the late 19th and early 20th century. The mill was destroyed by fire in the mid 1940s but the house still remains.

Burnley Road, Lineholme, 3rd July 1911. The present caravan site is on the right. Road-widening dramatically altered the appearance of this stretch of road, once known as 'Rutchley'.
In this picture, people are out to watch the demonstration of Lancashire Fire Brigades, an annual event held in a different Lancashire town each year. Todmorden was represented by the Corporation 'steamer', the accident ambulance and the fire brigades of the firms of Moss Bros, Wilson Bros and Varley Bros.
Members of the Cornholme Boys Brigade are collecting donations.

Lydgate and Harley Wood, from lower Cross Lee, 1910-12.
The view looks over Stoney Royd Lane. Harley Wood Church can be seen, far right, while Robinwood Mill dominates the valley in the distance.
Houses were built along Stoney Royd Lane in 1933. Advertised as 'The Owlers Estate', the three-bedroom semis were for sale from the contractor, J A Dufton, at £550 each. The Glen Estate, left, was developed for housing by the Council in the mid 1960s.

Fred Newell, with Dorothy Thewliss, haymaking at Stannally, 1978.
Born at Rake Hey in 1907, Fred was the youngest of seventeen children. As a boy, he helped his father on the farm, delivering milk every morning before school. At age twelve he went to work in the mill, then became an apprentice butcher, but for most of his working life he was employed on the parks, always farming in his spare time. Fred never retired in the conventional sense and in his later years could be found at Stannally, assisting the owners, Tom and Dorothy Thewliss.

All Saints Church, Harley Wood, 1905.
A couple, out for a walk with their young family, add a touch of human interest to this picture postcard view of Harley Wood.
Designed by local architect James Green, the church was opened in 1859 and served the whole of the Burnley valley until 1901 when Cornholme established its own parish. Not visible in this picture is the school which stood adjacent to the church. The school closed as a day school in 1957, and both church and school were demolished in 1975, the land redeveloped for housing. James Green also designed 'Hillside', the house seen here with the turrets, which he built for his daughters. He also designed the Stoodley Pike monument and the Burnley Mechanics Institute.

Coronation street party, Church Road, 1953.
Coronation Day festivities took place on a rain-sodden Centre Vale Park on Tuesday, 2nd June 1953. Street parties were held over to the following Saturday. Here on the Harley Wood pre-fab site, balloons have been strung between the buildings and flag-bedecked tables set out on the grass. On a special table are two large, iced cakes in red, white and blue, one of them topped with a model crown. The children are all ready to start – once the picture has been taken – on the jellies and cakes, the fruits of a combined operation by the mothers.

Robinwood Mill and the railway viaduct are predominant in this view of Lydgate, around 1910, however, the little boy commands our attention – one wonders whether he is there by chance or design.
Robinwood Mill was Fielden Bros' main spinning mill, employing some 300 work-people. Following closure in 1959, the mill was occupied for a few years by Thornbers Chicks before being taken by Wood Mac. A fire in 1992 destroyed a large part of the six-storey building.
The shop on the immediate right is the Lydgate branch of the Todmorden Co-op.

Harold Penney, photographed outside his fish and chip shop at 397 Burnley Road, 1904.
Though not nearly as numerous as they were before the war, fish and chip shops have endured with relatively little change. Evidently, 'Dabs' (fried, battered potato slices) were a local speciality then as they are today.
An contemporary advertisement for Penney's states that the shop was open 'Dinner, Tea & Supper Time' and supplied 'Fresh Tripe and Cowheels Daily'.

Photo-call at Riley Street, 1904.
This appears to be a post-election victory tour by the Liberal MP for Sowerby, John S Higham. In the by-election of 1904, Higham, a 45-year-old ex-Mayor of Accrington, was returned with a majority of 2,172 against the Conservative candidate, Simpson-Hinchliffe, of Cragg Vale. He held the seat for the next fourteen years.
It is unlikely however they stopped for a celebratory drink at the Riley Street Working Men's Club (seen in the background with the overhanging window), Mr Higham being a keen Temperance reformer. Having spent his boyhood in Cornholme, he was no doubt happy to be re-acquainted with the locals.

Former pupil revisits Lydgate School in 1954.
Lydgate School occupied the top floor of a three-storey building at the corner of Jumps Road: called 'Arch View', the rear of the building and school entrance (seen here) faced the railway viaduct. Originally a factory school run by the Fieldens, the school was transferred to the local School Board and closed in 1894 when Robinwood School was opened. The first headmaster was John Marshall who served for 22 years and was paid by the mill. Only two rooms were available for scholars, with two classes in the larger room and one in the smaller: 127 scholars in total.
Former pupil, John Fred Nuttall, seen here pointing, with Dr E Aitken-Davies, Education Officer, and H Horsfall, the manager of Robinwood Mill, reminisced about his schooldays and remembered being taught copperplate handwriting.

Bowed Row, 1972.
The curving terrace was built by Fielden Bros to house the workers of Robinwood Mill. The houses at the bottom end were back-to-back while those above the court were through houses. The whole property was built over the water course.
One night, in January 1976, during a heavy storm, the supporting culvert collapsed and one of the residents of Bowed Court plunged into the river. The following day, a number of the occupants were evacuated and rehoused. Half of the row was demolished, the other half remained for some time before eventual clearance.

Lydgate and Knotts, viewed from a point near to Eagles Crag, 1933-4.
Knotts Road is on the left, Robinwood Mill and dam at lower right.
Road improvement work had recently been carried out and a retaining wall constructed. The terraced houses along the main road, bottom left, were demolished in the early 60s.

Black Rock Garage, late 1950s.
Black Rock Garage was something of a landmark in its day, though it lasted for only eleven years. It was run by Ronnie and Margaret Stansfield (seen here), who moved from Blackshawhead to set up the business in 1955.
Ronnie did car repairs and servicing and they both served petrol. One of the downsides of owning the garage was that motorists would often knock them up during the night pleading, "We've run out of petrol."

Ingbottom, 1905-10.
Ingbottom is another place name which has all but disappeared, the word 'Ing', meaning field.
The place looks much as it does today, although without Vale Mill chimney. A bakers van is stopped outside the shop at the corner of Frieldhurst Road.
Topographical views such as this formed the staple subject for picture postcards in the pre-First World War period.

The Crabtree family, Roundfield Farm, c.1910.
This simple family portrait shows Sutcliffe Crabtree, on the left, with his wife Sarah, their daughter Martha Alice, and her husband Joseph William Shaw. Sutcliffe worked as a tackler at Vale Mill. His bye-name was 'Sut' o' Black Harry's', because his father, Harry Crabtree, who had been a fire-beater at Vale Mill, was known as 'Black Harry'. Joseph Shaw was a platelayer on the Cornholme-Portsmouth stretch of the railway. He died in 1932, aged 48. Marth' Alice died five years later at 47. The Crabtrees rented the property at the time. Situated on the upland edge above Black Rock, Roundfield was not easily accessible from the valley and has since become a ruin.

Vale Baptist Chapel awaiting demolition in 1967.
The 1960s saw the demise of many of the town's churches and chapels. In the Burnley valley, Vale, Shore, Lydgate and Lineholme Baptists chapels, Cornholme Methodist and Harley Wood churches, all fell victim to dry rot and falling membership. Some, like Vale, survived by transferring to their schools. Services continue today at Vale, the congregation strengthened by former members of Shore and Cornholme.
Vale was an offshoot of the parent church at Shore, a need for a place of worship in the valley recognised as population shifted in that direction. The chapel was opened in 1853 and enlarged in 1873 when a school was added. Within the burial ground is a memorial to the Cornholme writer and dialect poet, James Standing (1848-78).

For a few brief summers, Cornholmers enjoyed their own open-air bathing pool – a disused mill dam, called 'Varley's Pool', on the site of a former dyeworks behind Cornholme railway station. The pool was rented for a nominal fee by Tom Porter, a tackler at Joshua Smith's and part-time swimming instuctor, who set up the community swimming club. This group of family members and friends are pictured during the long, hot summer of 1933.
From the left, standing: Maud Fielden, Jacob Fielden, George Woodall, Eddie Mitchell, Harold Law, Joe Fielden and Wilfred Duffield. Seated: Mr Nuttall and Winnie Fielden.

The Mayor of Todmorden, Jeremiah Jackson, presents prizes at a swimming gala at Varley's Pool, Saturday 15th August 1934.
Organised by Tom Porter (on the right), the gala raised money for the Todmorden Society for the Blind, and helped to raise public awareness of the need for public baths. Janie Pickersgill, pictured here, came second in the neatest dive competition and won a set of cake forks.

Cornholme Mission Church – the 'Tin Tabernacle' – was established in 1894 in a corrugated metal building at the top of Lincoln Street, and served as both Church and Sunday school until the new parish church was opened in 1902. The mission was supported by the parishes of Holme-in-Cliviger and Harley Wood, from which the early congregation was drawn.

The members pictured here are, from the left, back row: William Coulton, Mrs Nightingale, unidentified, Tom Ingham, the next two unidentified. Middle row: Mrs Acornley, Emily Law, Jane Ellen Nightingale, Rev J. F. Marchant, Curate of Harley Wood, unidentified, and Sarah Ann Hollin. At the front: Alice Ogden and Alice Ann Banks. All the ladies were unmarried at the time.

The last Sunday service at the tin hut took place on 21st September 1902. The Sunday school was eventually re-housed in a new, brick building – the Whittaker Memorial School, which still stands today.

Laying the foundation stone of Cornholme's parish church, St Michael's Day, 29th September 1900. Laying the stone is Mrs Master-Whittaker, wife of the Vicar of Holme, who not only gave the site but bore the whole of the cost of the building.

The church was built on the site of the old Vale Bobbin Mill, directly opposite Vale Board School.

Cornholme Church and Vicarage, 1905.
Prominent in this view from Tongue Brink is the newly-completed vicarage, home of the first vicar of Cornholme, Rev O F Aston.
The Church of St Michael & All Angels was formally opened on 27th September 1902. Designed by the well known church architect, Hodgson Fowler, of Durham, the church was built in the style of English Perpendicular Gothic. A clock was added to the tower in 1903, a further gift from the benefactors, Rev and Mrs Master-Whittaker.

A Sunday School Anniversary procession from St Michael's Church, 1920s.
Headed by the banner, the procession wends its way towards Portsmouth, the Cornholme Brass Band in rousing support.
The banner also made an appearance on the annual Field Day, an event eagerly anticipated by all concerned. After processing through the village, the troupe would head for the field at Frieldhurst where races would be run, prizes competed for and unlimited buns and coffee served.

Cornholme, 1905-10.
Cornholme was a self-contained community where everyone knew each other, and from which people seldom travelled far. Between Ingbottom and Cornholme Waggon arch, at this time, there were some 40 shops. The village barber was William Bunt whose shop can be seen at right, with the barber's pole. His daughter, Susie, ran a ladies hairdressers upstairs. The building still stands, although the rest of Harrison Street was pulled down some years ago. The first shop on the left of the picture was Walton & Sutcliffe's, bakers and confectioners. All the buildings on the left still remain apart from the so-called Town Hall building, immediately before Frostholme Mill. This was demolished to provide parking for Alan Cooper's transport.

Weavers at Joshua Smith's, Frostholme Mill, enjoy a dinnertime break in the sunshine, 1940s. They are, from the left, Dorothy Shore, Eunice Snell and the twins – Florence and Georgette Jackson. Joshua Smith's ran the mill from 1882, employing at its peak over 700 workers. During the Second World War, the firm produced high quality cloth for barrage balloons so all the operatives were exempted from service. The main weaving shed was commandeered by the Ministry of Defence for the storage of shell casing. The owners were compensated for loss of profits and the shed reconstructed in 1947.
After Smith's, the mill became part of Fine Spinners & Doublers, of Bolton, then taken over by Courtauld's, before being bought, in 1971, by Alan Cooper Ltd, manufacturers of office furniture.

Gem Cinema usherettes, 1938. Vincent Lee took this shot of his wife, Doris (right), with her friends and work colleagues, Mary Hanley (left) and Annas Ormerod, at the rear of his newsagents shop in Cornholme.

The cinema, which had been re-opened as the Gem Picture Theatre in 1931, was in its heyday at this period, drawing hundreds of customers every night except Sundays.

Annas Ormerod, whose father owned and managed the Gem, had recently started a teaching career – she was teaching in Doncaster at the time – and was home on her summer leave. Like other members of the family, she was recruited to help out at the cinema. Annas later married and moved back to Todmorden, teaching at Roomfield, Walsden, Cornholme and Vale schools.

After the cinema closed in 1957, the building found a new use with Gem Precision Engineering. In 2005, it was demolished to make way for a new residential development.

Springwood Terrace, Pudsey Road, c.1910-12.
No information is available for this photograph but the picture was almost certainly taken at the request of the residents – possibly to commemorate an important event or occasion in their lives, or that of the community. Strangely, most of the menfolk are missing. The man leading the horse could be a family member.
Springwood Terrace was built in 1900 by Joseph Lord, of the Roebuck Inn. All the houses were tenanted at the time.

Woodbine Terrace, Pudsey Glen, c.1910.
The view is from Pudsey Road with Lishman & Company's offices (later Cornholme Working Men's Club) on the left. Lishman's Glen Dyeworks can be seen in the background.
The children standing in the street add some interest to this Cornholme street scene.

Pudding Lane, c.1910.
Pudding Lane was the access route from Cornholme to the upland farming communities of Shore and beyond. The road was notoriously difficult for vehicles in the best of weather, and it was not unusual to see funeral parties walking with their coffins to Shore. A proposal to build a new road was put forward at a public meeting in 1875 but nothing came of it.
Finally, in May 1921, Shore New Road was completed by Todmorden Corporation at a cost of £2,000, a large part of which was raised by public subscription by the local residents.
The cottages shown here were called Mawking Bottom.

A rural scene in the Pudsey valley, about 1920.
New Delight Farm and cottages are set against the backdrop of Reddish Shore Rocks. The house on the hill is Wood Cottage, and below this is a pair of cottages with the unusual name 'Doldrum'. The view has remained relatively unchanged although the land is no longer farmed.

Cornholme School Band, 1906.
The tin-whistle band are pictured with headmaster William Aspinall. The boy seated on left of the drum, holding the beater, is Percy Sutcliffe (1896-1977), a former Mayor of Todmorden. Percy left school to work in the finance department of Wilson Brothers, the local bobbin makers. In his early thirties became a self-employed stockbroker, working from an office at the Oddfellows Hall, Todmorden. During the 1914-18 era, the tin-whistle band would parade once or twice a week in Cornholme to the amusement of bystanders and the delight of proud parents. At school, the members of the band were always called in first from the playground, they would then provide musical accompaniment while the rest of the children marched in step to their respective classrooms.

Morning assembly at Cornholme School on the last day of term, 1979. Acting headteacher Donald Whitehead can be seen conducting the assembly.

The teaching staff of Cornhome Council School in 1929.
From the left: Tom Hodgins, Winnie Horsfall, Mary Townsend, John Bentley (headmaster), Herbert ('Manny') Wood, Ethel Ormerod (head of Infants), Alice Law and John Graham.
John Bentley left in 1931 to become Head of Roomfield Senior School. After the war, he and Miss Townsend were married.

Cornholme school children 'Dig for Victory', 1940.
During the early war years, everyone with a plot of land was urged to grow vegetables instead of flowers in order to become self-sufficient. Cornholme Council School headmaster, John Graham, turned this opportunity into a lesson for his senior pupils by renting this allotment behind Portsmouth railway station. Later he took another allotment that covered half of Portsmouth recreation ground and pupils from the two top classes were able to produce enough food for the entire school's dinners.

A march-past of auxiliary services during the early months of the war, 1939. Here, the ARP wardens are followed by the nurses and cadets of the St John Ambulance Brigade. Marching third from the right is Frank Helliwell, the organist at Shore Chapel.

The Cornholme Co-op, with manager Billy Law and shop assistants in the doorway, is fitted with regulation blackout facilities while place-names on the faschia board are conspicuously blanked out. Notices in the window give information about registration for food rationing.

None of the buildings seen here remain today - those in the background were part of Wilson Bros' bobbin mill complex. The co-op closed in the mid 1960s.

The St John Ambulance Brigade, once present at every public gathering, are no longer a presence in Todmorden.

Station Parade, Portsmouth, c.1910. Station Parade, a superior terrace of seven houses with a shop at each corner, was built in 1906 by Joseph Lord, of the Roebuck Inn.

Portsmouth Station, here without activity on what appears to be a Sunday afternoon, handled the freight for Cornholme's manufacturing industries which, at that time, included Joshua Smith's, Caldervale and Springwood mills, the shuttle shop, Wilson's bobbin mill, Carrfield mill and Pickles's. The goods yard was off to the left of this picture.

The bowling green, left, was a feature of the Roebuck Inn: a bowling club was formed soon after the green was opened in 1897 and remained active until 2004.

Eastwood Station, c.1905.
Due to the station's geographical position, the platforms were set diagonally apart, with a level crossing allowing access to the booking office, the down-side platform and the road to Higher Eastwood. A ramp, still in existence, gave access from the main road. The station closed for passengers on 3rd December 1951 but continued to receive coal until 18th May 1964.

A coal carter at Eastwood sidings. Coal was brought in by rail from the Yorkshire pits and tipped into chutes at three main collection points – Stansfield Road for Todmorden, Stubley for Cornholme, and Eastwood. The coal was weighed and carted direct to the mills, or to dealers' yards where it was distributed for domestic use. Eastwood supplied all the mills between Charlestown and Castle Street.

The site of the projected Sewage Disposal Works, Sandbed, 1901-2.
This early view of the construction site shows the river diversion work in progress. In November 1901, the contractors, Messrs W Jones & Co, of Manchester, suffered a crippling blow when a flood swept away their plant, leaving five months excavation work almost completely undone. The tender was then let to local contractor, Benjamin Lumb, who completed the works in 1908.

One of the first Vulcan cars, at Eastwood, 1902.
Not much is known about the early motor vehicles in the district but their appearance in the 1900s must have aroused considerable interest. The first non-commercial cars were made by local entrepreneurs with engineering backgrounds, such as Arthur Kinghorn, of Lord & Kinghorn, and Thomas Lord, of Sandholme Iron Co, who built two cars from scratch. In the earliest days of his motoring he had a man walk ahead of his car, waving a red flag to warn pedestrians.
This Vulcan, being admired outside the Station House Hotel, was built in Southport and had a 4 hp single cylinder engine and tiller steering. The driver is Alfred Horsfall.

Duke Street, c.1900.
This view of the Bridgeholme area takes in Duke Street, hidden from the main road by the railway embankment, Victoria Terrace in the middle distance, and Stoodley Lodge on the far hillside. At the turn of the century, the back-to-back houses at Duke Street were inhabited mainly by factory workers and their families, the larger house at the far end being the parsonage for Eastwood Congregational Chapel.
Over the years, Duke Street developed a reputation for being a less salubrious place to live and by the time they were demolished in the 1960s the houses were deemed to be unfit for habitation.

The Royal Oak Hotel, Springside, c.1967.
The Royal Oak, owned by Massey's Brewery, was a rather plain, nondescript pub in a row of 'double-decker' houses. The pub was referred to locally as 'Satan's Temple', perhaps because of its proximity to the Methodist Chapel across the road. The pub closed in July 1967 after which the entire block of property was demolished.

Lobb Mill and the railway viaduct, early 1900s.
This atmospheric view is from a position above the Horsefall Tunnel on the track leading to Rodwell End.
Lobb Mill takes its name from the spinning mill, centre, which became inoperative around the turn of the century. The razing of the chimney in September 1906 attracted photographers from miles around when the steeplejack offered a prize of a gold medal for the best picture of the chimney while falling. The event led to the formation of the local photographic society.
The chimney immediately behind Lobb Mill is that of Millsteads Mill which ended cotton production following a fire in November 1972.

Rodwell End Chapel, left, was built on the site of the first Baptist chapel in Todmorden (1703).
Baptism flourished here for some 80 years, then the chapel was used intermittently, first by the Baptists, and then by the Methodists who erected the present building in 1865.
As more mills, schools and chapels became established in the valley bottom the population gradually shifted in that direction and, by the early 1870s, the chapel had been abandoned in favour of Springside. It was eventually sold at auction at the Station House Hotel. Derelict and without a roof for many years, the building is now in the process of restoration for residential use.

Centenary of Todmorden Golf Club, May 1995.
Club Captain, Philip Brown, and Lady Captain, Val Cowie, with members in support, stage a re-enactment of the opening of the first links at Todmorden Edge in 1895, when the captain, F W Horsfall, 'teed-off' before a crowd of onlookers.
The club moved to the present site at Rive Rocks in 1907.

Higher Ashes, 1924.
With its adjoining cottages and outbuildings, Higher Ashes stands out prominently among its neighbours, occupying a commanding position off the Cross Stone-Blackshawhead road. A typical example of 17th century vernacular architecture, the house was probably built by William and Sarah Sutcliffe whose initials appear over the main porch with the date 1691. The Sutcliffe family were wealthy landowners who owned several properties on the Stansfield hillside as well as in Langfield. The same family also owned Stansfield Hall until 1851.
This picture shows Mrs Barritt whose family tenanted the farm from around 1900.

Castle Grove Methodists assemble on King Street for the annual Band of Hope Union demonstration, 1906-7. The 2 o'clock procession through the town would be joined by other Sunday school troupes, each headed by their banner. The demonstration – or gala – was normally held in the field in front of Woodlands.

The newly-constructed Castle Grove United Methodist Free Church, top left, replaced a much smaller chapel which stood alongside the railway on the opposite side of the street. The L&Y railway company made a grant of £610 and provided an alternative site so that they could demolish the old building. Castle Grove church finally closed in 1972.

Rugby Union played on the Sandholme ground, late 1920s.

The site between the river and the canal, near Castle Hill, was a shared playing field for cricket, football and rugby. Rugby was a winter sport and during the 1920s there were just three local teams – Todmorden, Bourillion and Calder Valley – competing in the Rochdale and Halifax Rugby Leagues. The old sports ground is scheduled to become a storage basin as part of the flood alleviation scheme.

The Castle Street area, viewed from across Woodhouse Bridge in the early 1900s.
Most of the properties on the north side of Halifax Road, including the three-storey Springfield Terrace, far left, and the chimney of Cinderhill Mill, have long since been demolished. Millsteads Mill, on the right, is still occupied industrially, at the present time by ABC Chemicals Ltd.

Woodhouse Mill, 1995.
Relic of a past industrial age, the fire-damaged mill stood derelict for several years before being rescued by local businessman and former demolition expert, Charles Moran.
Before the fire, in 1994, which gutted the interior and destroyed the roof and end wall, there were plans to turn the mill into a textile industrial museum. On the floors worst hit were a collection of cotton spinning mules imported from Bottoms Mill, Walsden.
Restoration and refurbishment of the Grade II listed building, carried out in consultation with English Heritage and the Victorian Society, was completed in 2003 with the release of 20 apartments, the first mill redevelopment scheme of its kind in Todmorden. The detached stone chimney was retained by the mill's previous owner, Robert Aram, as part of his collection of industrial monuments. This view from Cinderhill Road takes in the distant Langfield hillside and, far right, the settlement of Old Royd.

Causey Wood, 1890s.

Causey Wood Mill ('New Mill') was demolished around 1900 after standing empty for many years. Built for cotton spinning in 1826, it was first powered by water from Lumbutts Clough and converted to steam in 1833. The lower of the two dams fed a similar mill - Old Royd Mill - which also went into disuse but remained standing as a ruin until the 1920s.

When the mills were active there was no through road from Woodhouse and all traffic to the mills went via Old Royd. The row of cottages, known as 'Mouse Nest', was inhabited until 1960. The lower dam and Folly gardens became the site of the town's first municipal refuse tip. Now completed, 'the tip' has been transformed into a sports playing field. New Mill Dam remains, as an amenity for the local angling society.

The two cottages overlooking New Mill Dam were called Causey Wood View.

Croft Gate, Langfield, 1940s.
Croft Gate bears the earliest known datestone in the district: 1598 is carved on one of the door lintels.
The outside of the building has hardly changed, although the extension of 1707 has been enlarged in recent years. Until the 1940s, the interior was quite basic with a simple ladder giving access to the upper floor.
The man shaking the rug is George Sutcliffe who lived there with his family at the time. The Winfield family, who lived at Croft Gate in the early part of the century, ran a small shop and café in the built-on portion. Owen Winfield later became landlord of the Shepherd's Rest.

The Shepherd's Rest, Heyhead, 1920s.
The subjects are unidentified but they are most probably the landlord, Robert Coupe, and members of his family, who were tenants between 1922 and 1931.

Local farmers brave the weather for an auction at Height Farm, December 1982.
Pictured in the centre are father and son, Jack and Roy Starkie, of Royd Farm.
This picture marks the end of an era. Hill-farming as a way of life was on its way out. Farmers were being persuaded, through incentives, to give up milk production, the older generation were not being followed by their children, and the farms themselves were being sold as gentrified homes.
Height, situated under the lee of Stoodley Pike, is one of a small number of working farms in the area today.

Mankinholes, c.1902.
This view of the main street in the early 1900s is immediately recognisable. The men carrying jugs are probably villagers on their way to collect milk from a farm.

The 'Long Drag', Langfield Moor, 1920s.
Looking east from the Gaddings stone quarry along Langfield Edge, this view shows the old carriage road, said to have been made by the Fieldens to find work for their employees during the Cotton Famine of the 1860s.
The road runs from Heyhead on the Lumbutts Road, to Withens Gate, where it joins the Long Causeway leading to Cragg Vale.

A visit to Stoodley Pike in the 1930s.
Six men pushed a car to Stoodley Pike – whether for a bet, or a challenge, is not known – but this is the photographic evidence.
The exploits of young men who took on ridiculous feats for bets is legendary. These local lads borrowed the car – a Hispano-Suiza – from a factory owner friend in the Eastwood area.
The man in the dickie seat is Arnold Knight who lived at Callis Bridge.

# Acknowledgements

The pleasure of selecting and researching these photographs has been a real labour of love, but I could not have produced this book without the accumulated help of a great many people, too many to mention over the years, who have welcomed me into their homes and allowed me access to their photograph collections. To all of them my sincere thanks.

For permission to reproduce the photographs in this volume I am grateful to Shirley Anderton, Bill Barker, John Chadwick, Eunice Crossley, Geoff and Jean Dawson, Peter Eastwood, Greta Gill, Paul Greenwood, Jonathan Greenwood, Colin Holden, Ian Holden, Eddie Hartley, Valerie Hartley, Barry Lister, Glen Millhouse, Christine Newell, Dorothy O'Neill, Martin Parr, Tom Pilling, Jack Ratcliffe, Joan Rawson, Elsie Read, Arthur and Alice Stansfield, Margaret Stansfield, Peter Staroszczuk, Eunice Shaw, Barbara Shuttleworth, Mary Taylor, David Tempest, Whiteley and Dorothy Widdup, and Ian Ormerod-Wilkinson. Thanks also to Todmorden Photographic Society for allowing me to reproduce images from their archive.

I would particularly like to thank John Fielden for his support and for reading and suggesting improvements to my text; Tom Newell who helped me select photographs; and Barbara Diggle, Dorothy Dugdale, Violet Noble, Malcolm and Freda Heywood and Robert Priestley who were happy to share local knowledge and help track down information.

Finally, my warmest thanks to Glyn Hughes for his personal interest and for kindly agreeing to write the foreword.

# INDEX TO THE PHOTOGRAPHS

Adamroyd 58
Ambulance 70
Ashworth, Hubert 31
Auxiliary Fire Service 36

Bank Street 63
Barsby's 46
Bells, Christ Church 47
Birdcage Walk 14
Birks Bar 84
Black Rock Garage 103
Bob o' Stones 79
Boots chemists 11
Bottoms, Walsden 86-87
Bowed Row 102
Bowling greens 51
Bramley, Ruth 57
Bridge End Co-op 73
Britannia 50
Burnley Road 9, 11
Bus, Shade 73
Butchers, Shade 72

Calder College builders 45
Canal Yard 65
Carr Laithe 53
Castle Grove 120
Castle Street 121
Causey Wood 122
Chaffer sisters 79
Charter Day 17
Cheapside 66
Chew's Garage 64
Church Institute 13
Church Lads Brigade 29
Church Road 99
Church Street 14
Church Street and Strand 18
Cockcroft, Professor John 40
Co-op cart horse 19
Co-op, Dale Street 20-21
Copperashouse 76
Coronation street party 99
Cornholme 108
Cornholme Mission Church 106
Cornholme School 112-113
Cotton Queen 50
County Bridge 15
Crabtree family 104
Cricket team 90
Cricket, Schoolboys 49
Croft Gate 123
Crossley, Eunice 92
Crowther, Reuben 86
Currie, Dr 47

Dad's Army 37
Derdale 33
Dobroyd Road 61
Duke Street 117

Eastwood Station 115
Electricity cables 29
Ellis Wood's Astorians 21

Ferney Lee 54
Fielden Monument 62
Fire Engine trials 94
Fish and chip shop 100
Flood, Burnley Road 44
Flood, cricket ground 49
*Flying Scotsman* 78
Frostholme Mill 108

Gatley's 18
Gauxholme 74, 77
Gauxholme Fold 77
Gem Cinema 109
Gibson, Will 43
Golf Club 119
Greenlees, Thomas 16
Greenwood, Herbert 67
Grey, Dr 82

Halifax Road 22
Hallroyd Crossing 59
Harley Wood 99
Haymaking, Royd 55
Height Farm 124
Helliwell, Leonard 60
Higher Ashes 119
Highley's cloggers 39
Holebottom Mill 57
Holme, The 94
Home Guard 37

Ingbottom 103

Joshua Smith's 108
Jubilee Day procession 46
Julie Goodyear 23

Kettley, John 12
King Street, Fielden Square 63
Knotts Road 102
Knowlwood 7
Knowlwood United 90
Krazy Kuts 20

Lancs Fusiliers Old Comrades 51
Lanebottom 88, 89

Lanebotton 88, 89
Library 17
Lineholme 97
Lobb Mill 118
Long Drag, Langfield 125
Longfield Road 63
Lord Bros 30
Love, Geoff 41
Lovers Walk 53
Lydgate 100
Lydgate and Knotts 102
Lydgate School 101

Mankinholes 124
Maurice Wilson's 64
Meadowbottom Treat 56
Mons Mill 95
Motorcycle trials 78
Mount, The 55
Myrtle Street 25

National School 48
Navigation Inn 76
Naze Road 78
Newell, Fred 98
Newton Green 96

Oddfellows Hall 10
Old Comrades 51
Old Sinbad 32
Omega Street 24
Open Air School 93

Paolozzi's 42
Penney, Harold 100
Pilling's van 74
Portsmouth 114
Postmen 6
Procession of Witness 32
Pudding Lane 111
Pudsey Road 110

Ramsbottom, John 60
Recreation Ground, 54
Richmond Street 92
Ridgefoot, Burnley Road 42
Riley Street 101
Road paving 67
Road-roller 86
Rochdale Canal 34-35, 75
Rochdale Road 65
Rodwell End 118
Roomfield House 28
Roomfield School 26-27
Rose Street 24

127

Roundfield Farm  104
Royd, haymaking  55
Royal Oak  117
Royal Silver Jubilee  46
Rugby Union  120

Sager, John O  58
Salute the Soldier Week  37
Sam Tonkiss  53
Sandholme Ironworks  34
Sandholme Wharf  34
Sanger's Circus  94
Scaitcliffe Corn Mill  97
Scaitcliffe School  96
Schoolboys cricket team  49
Sewage Works  116
Shade  71, 75
Shann, Fred  69
Shaw House  28
Shepherd's Rest  123
Simpson, William  32
Smoke  54
Snowstorm  15
Sobriety Hall  25
Springside  117
Springwood Terrace  110
Stansfield Hall Lodge  5
Stansfield Hall Station  58
Stansfield family  63
Stansfield, Robert  79
Station Parade  114
Steele family  73
St Mary's Church  14
St Mary's C of E School  71
St Michael's Church  106-7
Stoodley Pike  125
Strand  18
Stuttard's wagon  43
Sunderland, George  35
Swimming gala, Cornholme  105

Taplin Memorial  10
Temperance Street  2, 24
Tennis  91
Todmorden Agricultural Show  50
Todmorden Orchestra  81
Todmorden Photographic Society  80
Tourist Information Centre  12
Train smash  59
Turner, Hilda  92

Union Bank  13
Unitarian charladies  68

Vale Chapel  105
Varley's Pool  106
Victoria Road  43
Vulcan car  116

Walsden aerial view  83
Walsden Carnival  87
Walsden horticultural class  85
Walsden Station  84
Walsden United  89
War Weapons Week  36
Waterside  68
Water Street  19
Wedding party  69
Wellfield Terrace  62
Whitham family  38-39
Wilkie's  23
Wilkinson, Sir Geoffrey  41
Williamson's  31
Wings for Victory Week  50
Woodbine Terrace  110
Woodhouse Mill  121
Woodpecker Inn  72
Worsley Cup  90